Why Is *That* in Tradition?

Why Is *That* in Tradition?

Patrick Madrid

Our Sunday Visitor Publishing Di\
Our Sunday Visitor, Inc.
Huntington, Indiana 46750

For my son
Timothy Killian,
with love.

"Heresies and certain tenets of perversity, ensnaring souls and hurling them into the deep, do not spring up except when the true Scriptures are not rightly understood and when what is not rightly understood in them is rashly and boldly asserted."

St. Augustine of Hippo
Tractate 18 on the Gospel of John

TABLE OF CONTENTS

INTRODUCTION

Several years ago, I was engaged in a public debate with a Protestant minister. The event was held at a Protestant church before a mixed audience of Catholics and Protestants. At one point in the debate, during the cross-examination section, my Protestant opponent posed this question to me:

"Can you give me one example of a tradition that's outside the Bible and is necessary for Christians?" He sat back with a smile, confident that I would not be able to answer his question.

"Yes, I can," I said. "It's right here." At that I dropped my Bible on the table in front of him with a thump.

No one in the audience moved.

My opponent blinked, apparently unsure what to say in response.

I explained: "The canon of the New Testament is a tradition, a Catholic tradition, that you as a Protestant follow." I continued, "The books that belong in the Bible, and in particular the New Testament, are part of Tradition. And you accept that Tradition and follow it, otherwise you would have no Bible — you simply would have no way of knowing what the Bible is unless you accepted the Tradition of the canon." Then it was my turn to sit back with a smile.

My Protestant debate opponent was no longer smiling. And for good reason. He had been caught in his own trap. His aim had been to trap me into offering an example of Catholic Tradition, something such as "purgatory" or "Mary's Immaculate Conception," that he could easily dismiss as, at the very least, not essential for a Christian believer to hold. That's what he expected me to offer as an example. What he didn't

9

expect was an example that he simply couldn't argue with. And even though, for the next few minutes, he did attempt to talk his way out of the jam he was in, the audience, and I (and, most of all, he himself, I think) realized with complete clarity that he had shot himself in the foot with that question: "Can you give me one example of a tradition that's outside the Bible and is necessary for Christians?"

The fact is, the canon of the New Testament is part of God's revelation to the Church. But that revelation didn't come to the Church in the pages of Scripture, the Written Word of God. Rather, this all-important information was gradually revealed by God to the Church completely outside of Scripture itself (after all, as I point out to non-Catholics, there is no "inspired table of contents" in the Bible telling us which books belong).

This revelation was preserved and faithfully taught by the Catholic Church, transmitted in its integrity from one generation to the next. That's why you and I have the same twenty-seven books in our copies of the New Testament — from Matthew to Revelation — that our Protestant, Mormon, and Jehovah's Witness friends have in theirs. They have these books in their Bibles because, like it or not, whether they are aware of it or not (very few of them are aware of it), they are accepting and adhering to a Catholic Tradition. And that's what made the question my debate opponent leveled at me so powerful. He was forced to see — in front of a large audience of Catholics and Protestants, no less — the reality of Catholic Tradition. He didn't admit that he recognized this fact, but everyone in the room did, and it was evident that he did too. It was a powerful moment.

You can take a cue from that episode and apply it to your own discussions with non-Catholics when the subject of Tradition comes up. Non-Catholics, especially Protestants, are conditioned to regard Catholic Tradition with deep suspicion. Tradition is a "red flag" word for many Protestants. They reject an appeal to Tradition because they believe Tradition equals "man-made doctrinal aberrations that have been added on to Scripture."

Let's touch on the subject of debates again briefly. Over the years, I've engaged in many public debates about religion with Protestants, Mormons, and others. Their arguments invariably include a strong condemnation of Catholic tradition — beliefs and practices they think are incompatible with Scripture.

"How can you Catholics believe in purgatory or the Immaculate Conception?" they ask with a roll of their eyes. "Those teachings are nowhere taught in the Bible. Worse yet, they're 'traditions of men' (cf. Matthew 15:1-9; Mark 7:1-13; Colossians 2:8; Ephesians 4:14), unbiblical teachings that go against what God says in the Bible." This attitude is common among Protestants, and you're likely to run into it, so it's important that you know what to say about Tradition: what it is, what it isn't, what it does, and why we need it.

For most Protestants, the word "Tradition" connotes the worst sort of man-made traditions, the kind Christ warned against in Mark 7:1-13 and Matthew 15:1-9, where he condemned those "traditions of men which nullify the Word of God."

Protestants see Catholic Traditions, such as the Eucharist, Marian doctrines, purgatory, and the like, as prime examples of man-made doctrines that conflict with biblical teachings. And since Protestants follow the Reformation principle of *sola scriptura*, they are all the more hostile to the Catholic teaching on the necessity and authority of Sacred Tradition. "Catholics have added things to their belief system that the Bible doesn't teach."

"Worse yet," they argue, "many Catholic traditions aren't simply additions to the Bible, they are in direct conflict with it." So you can see how important it is for us to examine here what Tradition is, as well as what it's not, and how Catholic Traditions are not at all in conflict with the Bible. Sound like a tall order? It is, yes, but it's actually something that, once you demonstrate, becomes a great help to Protestants coming into the Catholic Church.

To put it a different way, Tradition ceases to be a stumbling block, and becomes instead a steppingstone into the Catholic Church. Many converts to the Catholic Church have told me this was their experience, once they encountered a Catholic who was ready, willing, and able to explain what Tradition is (and isn't) and how to see that truth in Scripture itself.

My goal in this book is to help you help them see and accept Sacred Tradition for what it is — the Church's lived understanding of the deposit of faith, handed on faithfully and completely from one generation of Christians to the next. To accomplish that goal, we'll look not only at the meaning of these Traditions and traditional customs found in the Catholic Church, but we'll survey the writings of the Church Fathers and the early councils so that their own explanations will help us better understand *why* these teachings are part of Catholic Tradition.

But before we can help non-Catholics understand what Tradition really is, let's try to walk a mile in their shoes and see Catholic Tradition the way *they* see it.

i. Is Tradition Just a Game of 'Telephone'?

Remember in grammar school playing the game "Telephone"? The teacher would start the ball rolling by whispering a phrase into the ear of the first student — something like, "Tell Frank to come inside and wash his hands for dinner." Then the student would lean over and whisper that phrase into the ear of the kid next to him. And so on. Each student would get the phrase whispered to him and he, in turn, passed it on to the next one. Once the last student had been told the phrase, it was his job to tell the class out loud what he had heard. The funny part of the game is that whatever the last kid said was always different, usually wildly different, from what the teacher said. So, for example, the teacher's original message: "*Tell Frank to come inside and wash his hands for dinner,*" might come out the other end, garbled and strange, as, "*Tell Frankenstein he's eating frozen bats for dinner.*"

It's no wonder kids get such a laugh out of the "Telephone" game. The more bizarre the mistranslation of the original phrase, the better; that's what makes the game popular: to see just how garbled a message can get after passing through twenty or thirty people. It shows how easily and quickly corrupted the original message can become as it passes through the ears and minds and mouths of each intermediary whose job it is to pass along that information.

That game of "Telephone" is precisely how many non-Catholics, especially Evangelical Protestants, view Catholic Tradition. They see the Catholic Church's traditions as just so many examples of bungled, jumbled, erroneous understandings of the things that Jesus and the Apostles taught those of the early Church. And the reason they assume they are erroneous is because they assume that after two thousand years of transmission, from one generation of Catholics to the next, these traditions have become encrusted or even warped beyond recognition with human error.

Not too long ago, for example, I was conducting a parish apologetics conference, and during one of the breaks I got into a conversation with a young woman who was raised Catholic but who is now an ardent Evangelical Protestant. Just a few minutes into our discussion, the question of Tradition came up. Sure enough, she rolled her eyes with disdain at the very mention of "tradition." As if she were reading from a script, she asked me, "Do you remember the game in school called 'Telephone'? That is what Catholic tradition really is." (As you might imagine, I spent the next several minutes explaining from the Bible why that was not the case!)

It's amazing how widespread this misconception about Tradition is among non-Catholics, especially Protestants, Jehovah's Witnesses, and Mormons. They assume that any information given by Christ and the Apostles that wasn't written down in Scripture has been subjected to the same, if not worse, kind of distortions and inaccuracies as it was handed down orally, from one generation of Christians to the next.

This assumption is understandable, even if it's incorrect. All of us want to believe that the information we think we know about Jesus Christ and what he taught is accurate and not a distortion of the truth.

The key for the Catholic who wants to explain intelligently and convincingly that Tradition is not the same thing as the game of "Telephone" is to show that the way Catholics believe in a given Tradition today is the same as it was believed in the early Church.

By demonstrating through a comparison between current Catholic teaching and ancient Catholic teaching, using an issue such as baptismal regeneration or the Real Presence of Christ in the Eucharist, you can show that there has been no breakdown or distortion of the meaning of these doctrines over two thousand years of Christian history. And that is a stupendous characteristic of Tradition. It shows us that, indeed, Christ has been true to his promise that he would send the Holy Spirit to guide the Church into all truth (cf. John 16:12-13) and that he himself would be with his Church, "even until the end of the world" (cf. Matthew 28:20).

This is why the Catholic Church can speak with a confidence and an authority that is not, ultimately, her own: it's Christ's own authority that she speaks with. Just as he said, "Whoever listens to you, listens to me. And whoever rejects you, rejects me" (Luke 10:16; cf. Matthew 16:18-19, 18:18). St. Paul himself explains that he, as a member of the magisterium of the infant Church, had the obligation of making sure the Church understood the message in accordance with the *way in which* he had intended it to be understood:

> "Now I would remind you, brethren, in what terms I preached to you the gospel, which you received, in which you stand, by which you are saved, if you hold it fast — unless you believed in vain. For I delivered to you as of first importance what I also received, that Christ died for our sins in accordance with the scriptures . . ." (1 Corinthians 15:1-3, RSV).

That passage from St. Paul is a wonderfully compact theological mini-treatise on the nature and purpose of Tradition, as well as how it corresponds to Scripture and the magisterium. Let's do a brief analysis.

First, notice the words St. Paul chooses:
a. There is a body of teaching that "you have received" (Greek: *parelabete*);
b. Which "I preached" (Greek: *euangelion*);

c. You are to "*hold it fast*" to this body of teaching, meaning you are not permitted to neglect or dispense with this oral teaching;[1]

d. St. Paul "delivered" (Greek: *paredoka*) this teaching orally, and now, in his Epistle, he is reminding us to adhere to that orally delivered teaching;

e. This orally transmitted teaching corresponds with and complements the teaching of Scripture, just as it is a sure *interpretation* of what it reflects in Scripture (i.e., the inextricable linkage between Scripture and Tradition);

f. St. Paul reminds his readers that he, too, "received" this oral teaching first and then handed it on to them (which is the precise meaning of Tradition: receiving it, handing it on, etc.);

g. It is the role of the magisterium (Latin: teaching office; cf. Matthew 28:19-20), represented here by St. Paul, one of the Church's first bishops and Doctors, to explain the meaning of Scripture and faithfully deliver the message to the faithful.

Chapter 15 of 1 Corinthians provides us with an excellent biblical backdrop for understanding how it is that Tradition works in the Church alongside, and never in competition with, Sacred Scripture.

As we examine the many Traditions and traditions covered in this book (the "capital-T" Traditions and "small-t" traditions will be explained later), I hope one thing will begin to become clear: that these Traditions proclaimed by the Catholic Church today are not some kind of rabbits pulled out of a hat. They aren't "Catholic inventions," concocted by wily prelates in an effort to complicate the Gospel of Jesus Christ.

No. The Traditions proclaimed and taught by the Catholic Church come not from her but from her Lord. He entrusted these teachings to his Church and commanded her to go forth and teach them to all nations (cf. Matthew 28:20). In the earliest years of her existence, the Church carried out this mission in two ways: first, she orally preached and taught and handed on the deposit of faith in its entirety and in its integrity. And second, members of the magisterium — such as Paul, Peter, James, John, and other inspired writers — set forth the Church's teaching in writing, bequeathing to us the rich deposit of the Written Word of God, Sacred Scripture. Some of the teachings were explicit in Scripture (e.g., the Incarnation, the Atonement, the Resurrection, the Eucharist, and baptismal regeneration).

Some teachings, on the other hand, are contained in Scripture only implicitly. They are not explicitly told to us in the pages of Scripture. While we can rightly say that Scripture "contains" doctrines such as the Trinity or the Hypostatic Union or the communion of saints, we do so with the awareness that these teachings are implied by other teachings that are expressed.

For example, the expressed, clear biblical teaching that the Church is the Body of Christ (cf. Romans 12; 1 Corinthians 12) and that there is only one Body (not one on earth and another in heaven), combined with the expressed, clear teaching that physical death cannot separate us from the love of Christ or from unity with him in the Body of Christ (cf. Romans 8:35-39), leads the Church to make a necessary inference based on these explicit truths. Namely, that because those things are true, it implies another truth: that the communion of saints (i.e., our unity in and through Christ with all the members of the Body) is not reserved merely for this life on earth, but it includes all those, living and in heaven (or in purgatory), who are in the Body of Christ.

There is no doubt that this Catholic doctrine of the communion of saints was taught by the Apostles, even if only in a seminal form, for we can see evidence of it throughout the writings of the early Church Fathers. The doctrine of the communion of saints is a Tradition of the Church; it is present implicitly in the written form of Tradition (Scripture) and it is explicit in the oral form of Tradition (Sacred Tradition). Here we see the interplay between what we are taught in Sacred Scripture and how those teachings are lived out in the Church through her living Tradition, which is manifested par excellence through her sacraments, liturgies, and prayers.

The Church gradually was able to disseminate these priceless treasures of teaching among the various Christian churches, and eventually, she was able to codify and formalize these inspired writings into what we know today as "The New Testament."

Since the beginning, the Catholic Church has proclaimed and defended the deposit of Faith that was given to her by Christ and the Apostles. That deposit of Faith is incomplete if it is missing the oral Traditions that are part of it, as much as it would be incomplete if it were missing the written Traditions that form part of it. Our duty as Christians is to heed the words of St. Paul: "[S]tand firm and hold fast to the traditions that you were taught, either by an oral statement or by a letter of ours" (2 Thessalonians 2:15).

This book will aim to show you how to better stand firm and hold fast to Tradition and why you should.

ii. What Is Tradition?

Before we can properly answer the question posed by the title of this book, "Why is this or that teaching in Tradition?" we must first answer the deeper question "What is Tradition *itself*?"

Many people, Protestants as well as even some Catholics, are baffled by the Catholic Church's myriad of unique doctrines and customs. They hear Catholics speak about "Tradition," but can't tell with certainty what exactly these traditions are. "Where did these traditions come from?" they wonder. "Are they compatible with Scripture?" And perhaps most fundamentally, they ask, "Why are these doctrines and customs part of Catholic Tradition at all?"

The goal of this book is to answer those questions and give the needed explanations and background for many of the things we see in Catholic Tradition. First, keep in mind that Tradition is another word for what we Catholics call the "Deposit of Faith,"[2] the Gospel, or as St. Jude said, "The faith once and for all handed down to the saints" (Jude 3). Notice that the Greek term St. Jude used here for "handed down" (Greek: *paradotheise*; the root form being *paradidomi*) is a word from which we derive our English word "tradition."[3] St. Jude's reminder in this passage is that a particular body of doctrine, the "deposit of faith," was handed on to the Church from Christ and the Apostles.

Consider this analogy: An acorn is the same identical thing as the oak tree it grows into, even though they appear different. The same is true of Tradition (i.e., doctrine). It may have been expressed in terms or in ways that might seem removed or even different from how it is expressed in the life of the Church today. The Trinity doctrine is a good example. It was not nearly so well thought out in the second century as it is today, nor

19

was the precise theological vocabulary that the Church relies on today developed in those early years. This is why some people are perplexed when they see some Catholic Traditions or customs that seem much more ritualized or codified than they appear to have been in the early Church. Don't let that confuse or disturb you. Just as an acorn grows and develops into an oak tree and remains the same essential organism it always was, so too with Tradition in the life of the Church. It is a living tradition, so we can and should expect it to mature and amplify as we move through time.

A very important point to keep in mind here is that although Christ and the Apostles handed on to the Church a specific body of teaching, this deposit of faith is not static. It never changes, in the sense that doctrines are deleted or added, but there is an ongoing development of doctrine in the life of the Church. This refers to the Church's progress in more deeply and more clearly understanding the riches of the Gospel message, a progress that has continued since the time of the Apostles. This progress also extends to the various and changeable ways the Church may use to express the unchanging Tradition.[4]

In this development, no new doctrines or Traditions are added or "invented," but rather, the Church can infer truths with certitude from other truths that are explicitly taught in written Tradition (i.e., the Bible) or unwritten Tradition. For example, there are several explicit elements of divine revelation that are taught in Scripture and in the oral Tradition of the Church: (1) that there is only one God; (2) the Father is God; (3) the Son, Jesus Christ, is God; and (4) the Holy Spirit is God.[5] From these truths, and under the guidance and direction of the Holy Spirit who guides the Church "into all truth" (cf. John 14:25-26; 16:12-13), the Church was able to infer that if there is only one God, and the Father, Son, and Holy Spirit are each God, then the doctrine of the Trinity — one God in three Persons — is also true. It must be true, in fact, or else the revelations that there is One God, and that Father, Son, and Spirit are each true God become a jumbled mass of irreconcilable contradictions.

So, because, in the sense described above, doctrine "develops" in the Catholic Church (though it never changes or ceases to mean what it once did), the First Council of Nicaea (A.D. 325) was able to authoritatively define as dogma the doctrine of the Trinity. Now, Jehovah's Witnesses, Mormons, Oneness Pentecostals, and other aberrant religious groups will try to convince you that the Catholic Church "invented" the doctrine of the Trinity; that is not the case. The truth about the Trinity could not be "invented" by the Catholic Church — it had always been true, something revealed by God.

But some elements of revelation were delivered to the Church in explicit terms (e.g., the Virgin Birth of Christ; cf. Matthew 1:22-25; Luke 1:26-38), while some, such as the Trinity, were not. In both cases, the teaching comes from God, though in one case (the Virgin Birth) it was understood by the early Christians all at once, and in another case (the Trinity) it was only gradually perceived and eventually defined formally by the Church.[6]

One final point we can raise here about the development of doctrine is the analogy of a darkened room. Imagine you are seated in an entirely dark room. There's no light, so you can see nothing around you. Gradually, the light begins to come up and now you can see a few vague shapes around you: a chair over there, a couch against the other wall, a lamp next to the chair you're seated in, etc.

Soon, the light is bright enough that you can now begin to make out many more things in the room that you hadn't seen before. For one thing, you can now see that it's a large room. You see the vague outlines of a lot of chairs and couches. In time, the light is strong enough that you can see the color and texture of all the objects around you. Now you can recognize that certain things must be true as a result of the things you see in the room. You see large SALE price tags attached to the furniture, lamps, etc., you see a cash register at the far end of the room, and you correctly infer that you are sitting in a furniture showroom.

Nothing in the room explicitly says, "Hey, you're seated in a furniture showroom!" That fact is implicit in the things you can see. In other words, you're able to correctly infer that this implied truth (that you're sitting in a furniture showroom) must be true as an inference of what you know to be true about the objects in the room (i.e., they have SALE price tags). You can see here in this analogy two key things that pertain to Tradition and how the Church is ever growing in her knowledge and insights into it: First, the Church can correctly infer an implicitly revealed truth from one or more explicitly revealed truths. Second, going back to the darkened room for a moment, it's clear that the furniture, pictures, lamps, etc., in that room that were only fully visible once the light became strong enough for you to see them had been in the room all along. While you were sitting there in the darkness as the light grew, no one was adding furniture to the room. You were becoming better able to recognize those things that had been there all along. It simply took time and additional light for you to realize they were there.

This is a crucial issue to remember as you deepen your understanding of Tradition. There are some things in the Catholic Church's teaching that were formally defined well after the time of Christ and the Apostles. Don't let that throw you. Doctrines such as the infallibility of the pope, Mary's perpetual virginity, and the Trinity are not additions or inventions. They have always been part of God's revealed truth, though it took the Church time and effort to eventually understand them (cf. CCC 74-98; 2422).

In describing the purpose and function of the *Catechism of the Catholic Church* he promulgated, Pope John Paul II emphasized the crucial, unchanging role played by the magisterium of the Catholic Church in this two-thousand-year drama of handing on the authentic Tradition, the deposit of faith; a charge given to it directly by her founder, Jesus Christ (cf. Matthew 28:20):

> "A *Catechism* should faithfully and systematically present the teaching of Sacred Scripture, the living Tradition in the Church and the authentic Magisterium, as well as the spiritual heritage of the Fathers, Doctors and saints of the Church, to allow for a better knowledge of the Christian mystery and for enlivening the faith of the People of God. It should take into account the doctrinal statements which down the centuries the Holy Spirit has intimated to his Church. It should also help to illumine with the light of faith the new situations and problems which had not yet emerged in the past" (*Fidei Depositum*, subsection 2).

The universal *Catechism*, like the many authoritative monuments of Tradition that came before it through the centuries, is, as the pope describes it, a "statement of the Church's faith and of catholic doctrine, attested to or illumined by Sacred Scripture, the Apostolic Tradition and the Church's Magisterium . . . a sure norm for teaching the faith and thus a valid and legitimate instrument for ecclesial communion. May it serve the renewal to which the Holy Spirit ceaselessly calls the Church of God, the Body of Christ, on her pilgrimage to the undiminished light of the Kingdom!" (*Fidei Depositum*, subsection 3).

And this felicitous line from the pope points us to an essential characteristic of Sacred Tradition: light. This living Tradition is ever at work in the life of the Church; it is the way in which the Church lives out her understanding of the deposit of faith and passes it on — intact, unchanged, authentic — to each generation of Christians since the time of Christ and the Apostles. This Tradition, both written and oral, is, par excellence, the light of divine assistance that illuminates and guides the Church's path, as all of us in the Body of Christ make our common pilgrimage of faith toward the promised land of heaven.

iii. What the Bible Says About Sacred Tradition

First, let's dispense with the notion many non-Catholics have that all tradition is bad. This, of course, is nonsense. The Lord condemned bad "traditions of men" in Mark 7:1-13 and Matthew 15:1-9 because "they nullify the Word of God." He even singled out one of these corrupt, man-made traditions — the "Korban rule" — for special condemnation.

The Korban rule was a bogus legal loophole devised by some rabbis that allowed someone to technically deposit all his wealth in the temple as "alms," when in fact, he still had control over and access to his money. But this ruse allowed him to avoid having to help his parents in times of need, which directly contravened God's law to "honor your father and your mother" (Exodus 20:12). Christ rightly condemned this "tradition of men," precisely because it nullified the commandments of God.

For many non-Catholics, this is the end of the issue on the subject of Tradition, and they don't bother to look any further. And that's a real problem when the issue of Tradition comes up in discussions with a Catholic because the non-Catholic, especially if he is an Evangelical or Fundamentalist Protestant, rejects the notion of Tradition out of hand. Tradition is for him a "red flag" word that can only mean one thing: a man-made rule that goes against one of God's teachings. So Catholics need to point out that the Bible says a lot more about Tradition, showing that in addition to the bad traditions sometimes concocted by human beings, there are good Traditions and traditions (customs) — good because they come from God (in the case of Tradition) or because, though developed by men, they are helpful and completely in accord with God's commandments.

Let's start our examination of "Good Tradition" with this statement from St. Luke about the importance of non-written teachings that come to us in the Church:

> "Inasmuch as many have undertaken to compile a narrative of the things which have been accomplished among us, just as they were delivered to us by those who from the beginning were eyewitnesses and ministers of the word, it seemed good to me also, having followed all things closely for some time past, to write an orderly account for you, most excellent Theophilus, that you may know the truth concerning the things of which you have been informed" (Luke 1:1-4).

This vivid biblical passage is often overlooked in the discussion of Tradition. Notice that St. Luke is writing the Gospel account of Christ's ministry as a way to verify and attest to the truth "just as [it was] delivered to us by those who from the beginning were eyewitnesses." In fact, the Greek word for "deliver" Luke uses here is *paredosan* (from the root *paradidomi*), which is the verbal form for "to tradition" or "to hand on." St. Jerome translated this passage into Latin as, *"sicut tradiderunt nobis."* The Latin noun *traditio*, "tradition," stems from this root word, *tradere*.

We can see from St. Luke's teaching here that the truth about who Jesus Christ is and his message of salvation was already being preached and orally "traditioned" to the early Christians, Theophilus being one of them. He makes it clear here that one of the primary functions of Scripture is to testify to the truthfulness and authenticity of oral Tradition.

Now let's turn to St. Paul and see how he approached the subject of Tradition. First, in 1 Corinthians 11:1-2, he said: "Be imitators of me, as I am of Christ. I commend you because you remember me in everything and maintain the traditions even as I have delivered them to you" (later in that chapter, he explains in more detail one of those Traditions he handed on — the Real Presence of Christ in the Eucharist). Second, in 2 Thessalonians 2:15, we can begin to see more fully the nature of Sacred Tradition according to St. Paul's teaching:

"So then, brethren, stand firm and hold to the traditions[7] which you were taught by us, either by word of mouth or by letter" (2 Thessalonians 2:15, RSV).

These two passages show us that the body of doctrines given by Jesus Christ and the Apostles were intended by God to be transmitted to each generation of Christians. Some of these teachings have been codified in the written Tradition we know as Sacred Scripture, and others, even though they are at least implicitly or derivatively present in Scripture, are handed down in the Church through the medium of oral or "living Sacred Tradition."

These are the doctrines and dogmas of the Church that are not explicitly found in the pages of Scripture, but which are nonetheless part of the deposit of Faith (e.g., Mary's Immaculate Conception, her perpetual virginity, the infallibility of the pope, prayers for the dead, and the Mass as a propitiatory sacrifice, to name a few examples).

The second key thing to remember is that when the Catholic Church speaks about "Tradition," there are two possible meanings for the word. The first meaning refers to what I call "small-t" traditions that are man-made, not doctrinal in nature, and therefore are changeable, as the needs of the Church dictate.

These "small-t" traditions are the Church's customs and disciplines (such things as holy days of obligation, the pre-Communion fast, observance of the saints' feast days, and the different colored liturgical vestments worn by the priest at different seasons in the liturgical calendar). They were developed over time as the Church recognized their need, and because they are non-doctrinal in nature[8] they can be modified or even dispensed with altogether, as the Church determines. To reiterate, because these traditions are man-made, they are changeable.

But there is a category of Tradition that means something very different. These are the "capital-T" Traditions that are doctrinal in nature — and therefore unchangeable. Unlike customs and disciplines, these Traditions are not man-made; they are "God-made." They are part of the body of revealed truth given to the Church by Christ and the Apostles, as the

Holy Spirit inspired them to teach and explain these revelations. St. Paul spoke about this divine aspect of Tradition when he said:

> "Our exhortation was not from delusion or impure motives, nor did it work through deception. But as we were judged worthy by God to be entrusted with the gospel, that is how we speak, not as trying to please human beings, but rather God, who judges our hearts. . . . And for this reason we too give thanks to God unceasingly, that, in receiving the word of God from hearing us, you received not a human word but, as it truly is, the word of God, which is now at work in you who believe" (1 Thessalonians 2:3-4, 13, NAB).

What St. Paul means here is that when he and the other Apostles preached the message of Christ — the full Gospel — they weren't speaking of their own accord or delivering their own message. Rather, the Holy Spirit was inspiring them to preach and teach what he wanted them to preach and teach. As St. Paul explained, "All scripture is inspired[9] by God and is useful for teaching, for refutation, for correction, and for training in righteousness, so that one who belongs to God may be competent, equipped for every good work" (2 Timothy 3:16-17, NAB).

St. Peter echoed and amplified this truth about Scripture when he said, "Know this first of all, that there is no prophecy of scripture that is a matter of personal interpretation, for no prophecy ever came through human will; but rather human beings moved by the holy Spirit spoke under the influence of God" (2 Peter 1:20-21, NAB). This passage is particularly important when it comes to the issue of Tradition because of St. Peter's use of the phrase "human beings moved by the holy Spirit spoke under the influence of God." Notice that the inspiration of the Holy Spirit extended not merely to the words the human authors wrote on parchment (i.e., Sacred Scripture), but it also extends to their oral teaching — what they "spoke under the influence of God."

And this gets us to the very heart of the issue. "Capital-T" Tradition is actually a category with two parts, the written form of Tradition (which we know as Scripture) and the oral or unwritten forms (which we will discuss in more detail in later sections of this book). Once again, St. Paul points to this twofold aspect of Tradition when he said: "[S]tand firm and hold fast to the traditions that you were taught, either by an oral statement or by a letter of ours" (2 Thessalonians 2:15). The deposit of faith, as delivered by Christ and the Apostles, can rightly be understood in one sense as "Tradition" in its entirety. Some of that Tradition was handed on to us in Scripture; some of it was not.

That second mode of transmitting revelation within the Church came through oral teaching and was codified and lived out in the life of the Church through her prayers, sacraments, and liturgies, most particularly in the Divine Liturgy, known in the Western Church as the Holy Sacrifice of the Mass. But over time, the term Tradition came to be associated more strictly with those doctrines that are only implicit at best in Scripture and that were transmitted to each successive generation of Christians orally and outside of Scripture (cf. CCC 80-82).

The key to understanding Tradition is to realize that it really is not so much a separate thing apart from Scripture, but rather, it is the Church's *lived understanding* of the deposit of faith as set forth in the pages of Scripture. There was a wide agreement among many of the Church Fathers and Doctors that in a particular sense Scripture could be understood as "sufficient" in all things necessary for salvation. This means that, at least in a material sense, Sacred Scripture contains in itself the entire deposit of faith, explicitly or implicitly. Some of the teachings of the Church are not explicitly stated in Scripture, but they are, nonetheless, implicitly contained there by way of inferences and deductions we can make regarding what is implied on the basis of what is formally expressed. To put it a different way, the doctrine of the Immaculate Conception is nowhere explicitly taught in Scripture. But it is implied in many places. So the Church does not point to a particular passage of Scripture to say, "This passage proves the doctrine of the Immaculate Conception," but claims that the passage strongly implies it.

To use another example, the doctrine of the Blessed Trinity is not formally expressed in the pages of Scripture: One God in Three Persons. However, we can rightly infer that doctrine on the basis of those truths that are explicitly stated in Scripture; namely, that there is only One God, that the Father is God, the Son is God, and the Holy Spirit is God. On the basis of these explicit truths we can infer another truth — the triune nature of the One True God — that is indeed contained in Scripture, but only implicitly.

And this brings us to another major issue that every Christian must face: We must accept Sacred Scripture on God's terms, not our terms. In the Bible we read the phrase "Speak, Lord, your servant is listening" (1 Samuel 3:9). But so often, human beings adopt the "Listen, Lord, your servant is speaking" approach to the Bible. Many people take up the Bible with preconceived notions about what it teaches and they labor to wring a particular teaching from it, even if that means distorting its true meaning.

You can see this tragic problem everywhere: Mormons distort Scripture in an attempt to prove that there are many gods. Jehovah's Witnesses distort Scripture in an attempt to prove that Jesus Christ is not God. Evangelical Protestants distort Scripture in an attempt to prove that they have an absolute assurance of salvation, or in an attempt to prove the erroneous notion that Christians should go by the Bible alone (Latin: *sola scriptura*). You can see the problem. Any given group will pick up Scripture and try to make it say what they want it to say, even though it doesn't say that.

This danger of distorting the meaning of Scripture is why St. Peter warned, "[O]ur beloved brother Paul wrote to you according to the wisdom given him, speaking of this as he does in all his letters. There are some things in them hard to understand, which the ignorant and unstable twist to their own destruction, as they do the other scriptures" (2 Peter 3:15-16).

So, this should remind us that when we approach Scripture, we have to do so with a docility and a sincere desire to understand the authentic meaning of the text, the meaning the Holy Spirit wants us to receive from it. Anything other than the correct understanding of a given passage will lead to confusion and doctrinal ruin. This is precisely why St. Augustine warned:

> "If we read even in the divine Scriptures about hidden things and things most removed from our eyes, it will be possible, saving always the faith which fills us, to formulate any such opinion which, were the truth to be sought more carefully, might afterwards be found unsound [i.e., incorrect], and lest we might be found in error by our attempting to establish *what is but our own view, and not that of the divine Scriptures*, as if we would wish our [own] view to be that of the Scriptures, whereas we ought

to wish that the view of the Scriptures [i.e., the authentic *meaning* of the sacred text] should become our own" (*The Literal Interpretation of Genesis* 1:18-37, inter A.D. 401-415; emphasis mine).

In light of that wise counsel from St. Augustine and St. Peter, we'll conclude this introductory section on what Tradition is and how it functions in the Church with a particularly illuminating quote from the *Catechism*:

"The Tradition here in question comes from the apostles and hands on what they received from Jesus' teaching and example and what they learned from the Holy Spirit. The first generation of Christians did not yet have a written New Testament, and the New Testament itself demonstrates the process of living Tradition.

"Tradition is to be distinguished from the various theological, disciplinary, liturgical, or devotional traditions, born in the local churches over time. These are the particular forms, adapted to different places and times, in which the great Tradition is expressed. In the light of Tradition, these traditions can be retained, modified or even abandoned under the guidance of the Church's magisterium" (CCC 83).

iv. Examples of Oral Tradition Mentioned in the New Testament

Matthew 2:23 — "He Shall Be Called a 'Nazarene' "
St. Matthew tells us that when the Christ Child was still a toddler, the Holy Family returned from their sojourn in Egypt so "that what was spoken by the

prophets might be fulfilled, 'He shall be called a Nazarene' " (Matthew 2:23). This is a remarkable passage because there is no place in the Old Testament where this prophecy, "He shall be called a Nazarene," is recorded.

Under the inspiration of the Holy Spirit, St. Matthew was invoking an authoritative oral tradition about a prophecy that was fulfilled in Christ. Furthermore, it seems clear that he was placing this particular oral Tradition on par with the written Traditions (i.e., Old Testament writings), which he also quotes (sometimes as he quotes Christ, who is citing Scripture) and identifies to show their fulfillment in Christ (cf. Matthew 1:22-23; 2:15; 4:4).

Also, it's clear from the phrase "what was spoken by the prophets" that St. Matthew knew of the oral Tradition that had been handed down, and he knew his first-century Jewish audience would know of that tradition as well. He mentions this prophecy in an almost matter-of-fact way, knowing that his readers would know exactly what he was talking about. And they did. And the reason they did was clearly that they had been taught this prophecy as it had been spoken by the prophets centuries earlier, receiving it through the oral tradition of the Old Testament priests and teachers.

Matthew 23:2 — The 'Chair' of Moses

Again we see an oral Tradition from the Old Testament era being invoked as authoritative and binding — and this time Christ himself invokes it! Immediately before he issues a chilling condemnation of the corrupt conduct of the Pharisees, he reminds his listeners that even though the Pharisees were hypocrites ("white-washed tombs full of dead men's bones," etc.), they still possessed an authentic teaching authority

33

that they had received from Moses himself. This authority was symbolized as a stone seat:

"The scribes and the Pharisees have taken their seat on the chair of Moses. Therefore, do and observe all things whatsoever they tell you, but do not follow their example. For they preach but they do not practice" (Matthew 23:2-3, NAB).

This authority symbol, the chair of Moses, is nowhere mentioned in the Old Testament, yet Christ clearly regarded it as a binding tradition, or else he would not have made this startling statement. The chair of Moses was an Old Testament-era Tradition that was handed down orally, not through Scripture.

1 Corinthians 10:4 — The 'Rock' That Followed the Israelites

Here's another amazing example of an Old Testament Tradition being invoked in an authoritative way. St. Paul, referring to the Jews' forty years of wandering in the Sinai Desert, says:

"I do not want you to be unaware, brothers, that our ancestors were all under the cloud and all passed through the sea, and all of them were baptized into Moses in the cloud and in the sea. All ate the same spiritual food, and all drank the same spiritual drink, for they drank from a spiritual rock that followed them, and the rock was the Christ" (1 Corinthians 10:1-4, NAB).

By saying "the rock that followed them in the desert was Christ," St. Paul here invoked another oral Tradition that is nowhere recorded in the Old Testament. All we can know from what is recorded there (cf. Exodus 17:1-7 and Numbers 20:2-13) is that Moses struck a rock with his staff and the rock poured forth water.

No mention is made of the rock moving, much less following the Israelites. What's more, St. Paul invokes this oral tradition as a way to authoritatively interpret Scripture. This is a good example of how it is that oral Tradition is shown forth as the Church's lived interpretation of Scripture, the written portion of the deposit of faith.

2 Timothy 3:8 — Pharaoh's Court Magicians

Here St. Paul mentions, almost offhandedly, that "Janes and Jambres" were the names of the two magicians in Pharaoh's court when Moses changed his staff into a snake. But where did St. Paul come by this information? Not in Scripture, for their names are nowhere recorded. But apparently this too had been preserved in some oral tradition that St. Paul referred to in his letter.

Jude 9 — St. Michael the Archangel versus the Devil

> "Yet the archangel Michael, when he argued with the devil in a dispute over the body of Moses, did not venture to pronounce a reviling judgment upon him but said, 'May the Lord rebuke you!'" (Jude 9, NAB).

This encounter between St. Michael the Archangel and Satan is also not mentioned in the Old Testament. It was handed on through oral Tradition, and St. Jude obviously was familiar with it, as we can assume his readers were also.

Interestingly, this scriptural passage (and it is the Old Testament oral tradition that obviously preceded it) is the foundation of another Catholic tradition — the very popular "Prayer to St. Michael," composed by Pope Leo XIII (1878-1903) and picked up very quickly by Catholics around the world as a prayer for protection in times of danger, physical and spiritual. For decades it was read at the conclusion of all Masses celebrated in the Roman Rite. Although this practice has fallen into disuse at Mass, one can only hope and pray that this wonderful tradition will soon be revived.

The "Prayer to St. Michael" provides an excellent, compact summary of the theological truths contained in Jude 9:

"St. Michael the Archangel, defend us in battle. Be our safeguard against the wickedness and snares of the devil. May God rebuke him, we humbly pray, and do thou, O prince of the heavenly host, by the power of God, thrust into hell Satan and all the evil spirits who roam about the world, seeking the ruin of souls. Amen."

This prayer, even though it is of recent origin, is an excellent example of a "small-t" tradition. It is not doctrinal in itself, and so it can be modified or even dispensed with altogether, should the Church see a reason to do so (though that seems so unlikely as to be impossible). But it points us to the theological principle that it is God and God alone who will defeat the Evil One. Through prayer and fasting (cf. Mark 9:29),[10] we can defend ourselves and others against demonic aggression — just as the Blessed Virgin Mary and the saints in heaven can also help defend the Body of Christ through their intercessory prayers. But, as Scripture reminds us, "Our help is in the name of the LORD" (Psalm 124:8, RSV). Ultimately, the one who will "crush the head of the serpent" (cf. Genesis 3:15) is Jesus Christ, offspring of the "Woman" (cf. Revelation 12:1-18).

This tradition reminds us that even St. Michael himself, the most powerful of the archangels, turns to God as the ultimate victor in the war against evil and the

Evil One. We echo St. Michael's own words recorded in Jude 9 when we pray, "May God rebuke him!"

v. Examples of Oral Tradition and Customs Not Explicit in Scripture

When the Council of Trent (1545-1563) dealt with the question of Sacred Tradition, as it relates to Scripture, it did not furnish a list of extra biblical Traditions, mainly because there was a concern among the bishops that to do so would give the incorrect appearance that the list was "complete." But we can see many examples of Traditions that are only implicit in Scripture (remember the analogy of sitting in the darkened furniture showroom?), yet they are explicit in the life of the Church. These Traditions are seen in the Church's liturgies and prayers, its practices of such things as infant baptism and confession to a priest, the administration of the sacraments in general, the canon of Scripture, etc.

Here is a partial list of examples of these Traditions and traditional customs that are not explicit in Scripture but which Christians have believed and observed since the early years of the Church. The reference after each one shows just one or two examples of many that could be cited for each entry as evidence of an authoritative voice in the early Church[11] teaching the issue in question. These examples are intended simply to show the antiquity of these Catholic Traditions and customs:

Observing the Sabbath on Sunday (cf. St. Dionysius of Alexandria, died A.D. 265, *Epistle to Basilides*).
The Trinity: One God in Three Coequal, Consubstantial Persons (cf. Theophilus of Antioch, *To*

37

Autolycus, A.D. 180; Tertullian, *On Modesty*, circa A.D. 260; First Council of Nicaea, A.D. 325).

Praying for the Repose of the Souls of the Faithful Departed (cf. St. Cyprian of Carthage, *Letter 51*, A.D. 253; St. Cyril of Jerusalem, *Catechetical Lectures*, A.D. 350; St. Augustine, *On the Care to Be Had for the Dead*, A.D. 421).

Honoring Mary and the Saints (cf. St. Ephraim the Syrian, *Commentary on Mark*, A.D. 370; St. Basil the Great, *The Liturgy of St. Basil*, A.D. 373).

Infant Baptism (cf. St. Irenaeus, *Against Heresies* 2:22; St. Hippolytus of Rome, *The Apostolic Tradition* 21; St. Augustine, *On Baptism, On the Baptism of Infants*).

The Catholic Church Is the One True Church (cf. St. Clement of Alexandria, *The Instructor of Children*, A.D. 202; St. Cyprian of Carthage, *On the Lapsed*, A.D. 250).

The Pope and the Magisterium of the Catholic Church Are Infallible[12] in Their Teaching (cf. St. Irenaeus of Lyons, *Against Heresies*, circa A.D. 180–199; Tertullian, *The Demurrer Against the Heretics*, A.D. 200; St. Cyprian of Carthage, *Epistle to [Pope] Cornelius*, A.D. 252).

Each of Us Has a Guardian Angel (St. Clement of Alexandria, *Miscellanies*, A.D. 202; Origen, *Homilies on Luke*, A.D. 233).

HOW TO USE THIS BOOK

This book, like its companion volume — *Where Is That in the Bible?* — is not intended to be an exhaustive or scholarly presentation of the evidence for Catholic Traditions and customs. Rather, it's designed to be a popular-level handbook used for quick reference.

There is a vast amount of additional information that could have been given for each entry in this volume, but what you'll find here is, instead, the basic overview of a given Tradition that will get you started on your study. Since most people are not scholars, the goal of this book is to give them the basics so that they'll be encouraged to dig deeper into the more comprehensive works that can discuss these issues in greater depth. At the back of this book I provide a reading list that can help in that pursuit.

I recommend you use this book in conjunction with *Where Is That in the Bible?*[13] because that volume will provide you with plenty of scriptural evidence that parallels the historical and patristic evidence you'll find here.

Also, this book is not intended to replace your study of the *Catechism of the Catholic Church* and Scripture. Quite the opposite! Those two rich sources of Catholic teaching are indispensable for today's Catholic and interested non-Catholics. *Why Is That in Tradition?* is a reference tool that can help you delve deeper into the Church's treasury of doctrine and customs. In fact, all the issues discussed in this book are easily located in the *Catechism*, which in turn will provide you with the related verses in Scripture and the writings of the early Church that wonderfully round out your understanding of Catholic teaching. Make it a regular, consistent part of your daily life to read Sacred Scripture and the *Catechism*, even if only for ten or fifteen minutes a day. If you do so, then this book will be really able to help you in the way it's intended to.

The information presented here is mainly the historical background and evidence for Catholic Traditions and traditions. Often, the writings of the early Church Fathers are cited as examples, or "monuments," of Tradition. These authoritative Catholic witnesses from the early centuries of Christianity (e.g., St. Ignatius, St. Clement of Rome, St. Justin Martyr, St. Irenaeus, St. Cyprian, and St. Augustine) are very helpful in demonstrating and explaining why a given Tradition or custom is part of Catholic teaching.

For example, examining what St. Augustine teaches about the early Christian doctrinal Tradition of praying for the repose of the souls of deceased Christians (cf. Augustine, *On the Care That Should Be Had for the Dead*, A.D. 421) provides us not simply with a window into early Christianity and how it understood such things as prayers for the dead, it also comes to us from an authoritative source — from a major bishop who exerted an immense influence and authority, then as now.

Since so much of what we can know about the early Church comes from the teaching documents left by the various ecumenical councils, as well as from the treatises penned by many Church Fathers, this book will rely heavily on both sources to give answers to the question "Why is that in Tradition?"

The reader, incidentally, will notice that each section of this book includes a variety of quotations from the early Church Fathers. This field of study is known as "patristics" (Latin: *pater* = father), and innumerable excellent collections of the Greek and Latin writings of the early Church Fathers have been compiled, many now in English. The numerical references included in the citations in this book generally follow this format: for example, 12:7; the first number refers to the chapter number and the second refers to the paragraph or section number. In instances where three numbers are shown (e.g., 12:7:3) the reference indicates *book* (12), *chapter* (7), and *section* or *paragraph* (3).

While many scholars endeavor to adhere to the numbering system laid out by the preeminent nineteenth-century Catholic patristics scholar Jacques-Paul Migne (1800-1875), some variations in numbering have crept in, resulting in a difference in numbers among various collections.

I. AUTHORITY

1. The Primacy of Peter and His Successors

Perhaps the most undeniable element of authority in the early Church was its reliance upon the bishop of Rome, chosen the successor of St. Peter, as the focal point of unity in the Christian Church. The early Christians recognized that the bishop of Rome had a special primacy of jurisdiction and teaching authority, and these excerpts from the writings of the Church Fathers, including some from popes themselves, are striking examples of the wealth of evidence that exists to demonstrate this point. One thing worth keeping in mind as you read through these quotations: the constant and universal assertions from early Christian writers about the authority of the pope, as well as assertions to that effect made by the popes themselves, were never shouted down by other "orthodox" Christians. In other words, the very fact that there were such uncontested claims and recognition of papal primacy, emanating from bishops in the East as well as in the West, shows that the doctrine of papal primacy was not a later "Catholic invention" but was understood as a Tradition that came directly from Christ[14] and the Apostles.

Pope St. Clement of Rome, circa A.D. 80 — "Through countryside and city [the apostles] preached, and they appointed their earliest converts, testing them by the Spirit, to be the bishops and deacons of future believers. Nor was this a novelty, for bishops and deacons had been written about a long time earlier. . . . Our apostles knew through our Lord Jesus Christ that there would be strife for the office of bishop. For this reason, therefore, having received perfect foreknowledge, they appointed those who have already been mentioned and afterwards added the further provi-

44

sion that, if they should die, other approved men should succeed to their ministry" (*Letter to the Corinthians* 42:4–5, 44:1–3).

Hegesippus, A.D. 180 — "When I had come to Rome, I [visited] Anicetus, whose deacon was Eleutherus. And after Anicetus [died], Soter succeeded, and after him Eleutherus. In each succession and in each city there is a continuance of that which is proclaimed by the Law, the Prophets, and the Lord" (*Memoirs* 4:22:1).

St. Irenaeus of Lyons, A.D. 189 — "It is possible, then, for everyone in every church, who may wish to know the truth, to contemplate the Tradition of the Apostles which has been made known to us throughout the whole world. And we are in a position to enumerate those who were instituted bishops by the apostles and their successors down to our own times, men who neither knew nor taught anything like what these heretics rave about" (*Against Heresies* 3:3:1).

St. Irenaeus of Lyons — "But since it would be too long to enumerate in such a volume as this the successions of all the churches, we shall confound all those who, in whatever manner, whether through self-satisfaction or vainglory, or through blindness and wicked opinion, assemble other than where it is proper, by pointing out here the successions of the bishops of the greatest and most ancient church known to all, founded and organized at Rome by the two most glorious Apostles, Peter and Paul — that church which has the Tradition and which comes down to us after having been announced to men by the apostles. For with this Church, because of its superior origin, all churches must agree, that is, all the faithful in the whole world. And it is in her that the faithful everywhere have maintained the Apostolic Tradition" (*Against Heresies* 3:3:2).

St. Irenaeus of Lyons — "Polycarp also was not only instructed by apostles, and conversed with many who had seen Christ, but was also, by apostles in Asia, appointed bishop of the Church in Smyrna, whom I also saw in my early youth, for he tarried [on earth] a very long time, and, when a very old man, gloriously and most nobly suffering martyrdom, departed this life, having always taught the things which he had learned from the apostles, and which the Church has handed down, and which alone are true. To these things all the Asiatic Churches testify, as do also those men who have succeeded Polycarp down to the present time" (*Against Heresies* 3:3:4).

St. Irenaeus of Lyons — "Since therefore we have such proofs, it is not necessary to seek the truth among others which it is easy to obtain from the Church; since the apostles, like a rich man [depositing his money] in a bank, lodged in her hands most copiously all things pertaining to the truth, so that every man, whosoever will, can draw from her the water of life. . . . For how stands the case? Suppose there arise a dispute relative to some important question among us, should we not have recourse to the most ancient churches with which the apostles held constant conversation, and learn from them what is certain and clear in regard to the present question? . . . [I]t is incumbent to obey the presbyters who are in the Church — those who, as I have shown, possess the succession from the apostles; those who, together with the succession of the episcopate, have received the infallible charism of truth, according to the good pleasure of the Father. But [it is also incumbent] to hold in suspicion others who depart from the primitive succession, and assemble themselves together in any place whatsoever, either as heretics of perverse minds, or as schismatics puffed up and self-pleasing, or again as hypocrites, acting thus for the sake of lucre and vain-glory. For all these have fallen from the truth" (*Against Heresies* 4:26:2).

St. Irenaeus of Lyons — "The true knowledge is the doctrine of the apostles, and the ancient organization of the Church throughout the whole world, and the manifestation of the body of Christ according to the succession of bishops, by which succession the bishops have handed down the Church which is found everywhere" (*Against Heresies* 4:33:8).

Tertullian, A.D. 200 — "[The Twelve Apostles] founded churches in every city, from which all the other churches, one after another, derived the tradition of the faith, and the seeds of doctrine, and are every day deriving them, that they may become churches. Indeed, it is on this account only that they will be able to deem themselves apostolic, as being the offspring of apostolic churches. Every sort of thing must necessarily revert to its original for its classification. Therefore the churches, although they are so many and so great, comprise but the one primitive church, [established] by the apostles, from which they all [come forth]. In this way all are primitive, and all are apostolic, while they are all proved to be one in unity by their peaceful communion . . ." (*Demurrer Against the Heretics* 20).

Tertullian — "But if there be any [heresies] which are bold enough to plant [themselves][15] in the midst of the apostolic age, that they may thereby seem to have been handed down by the apostles, because they existed in the time of the apostles, we can say: Let them produce the original records of their churches; let them unfold the roll of their bishops, running down in due succession from the beginning in such a manner that [their first] bishop shall be able to show for his ordainer and predecessor some one of the apostles or of apostolic men — a man, moreover, who continued steadfast with the apostles. For this is the manner in which the apostolic churches transmit their registers: as the church of Smyrna, which records that Polycarp was placed therein by John; as also the church of Rome, which makes Clement to have been ordained in like manner by Peter" (*Demurrer Against the Heretics* 32).

St. Cyprian of Carthage, A.D. 253 — "[T]he Church is one, and as she is one, cannot be both within and without. For if she is with [the heretic] Novatian, she was not with [Pope] Cornelius. But if she was with Cornelius, who succeeded the bishop [of Rome], Fabian, by lawful ordination, and whom, beside the honor of the priesthood, the Lord glorified also with martyrdom, Novatian is not in the Church; nor can he be reckoned as a bishop, who, succeeding to no one, and despising the evangelical and apostolic tradition, sprang from himself. For he who has not been ordained in the Church can neither have nor hold to the Church in any way" (Letter 75, *To Magnus, On Baptizing the Novatians* 3).

St. Jerome, A.D. 396 — "Far be it from me to speak adversely of any of these clergy who, in succession from the apostles, confect by their sacred word the Body of Christ and through whose efforts also it is that we are Christians" (Letter 14, *To Heliodorus, Monk* 8).

St. Augustine of Hippo, A.D. 397 — "[T]here are many other things which most properly can keep me in [the Catholic Church's] bosom. The unanimity of peoples and nations keeps me here. Her authority, inaugurated in miracles, nourished by hope, augmented by love, and confirmed by her age, keeps me here. The succession of priests, from the very see of the Apostle Peter, to whom the Lord, after his resurrection, gave the charge of feeding his sheep [John 21:15-17], up to the present episcopate, keeps me here. And last, the very name Catholic, which, not without reason, belongs to this Church alone, in the face of so many heretics, so much so that, although all heretics want to be called 'Catholic,' when a stranger inquires where the Catholic Church meets, none of the heretics would dare to point out his own basilica or house" (*Against the Letter of Mani Called 'The Foundation'* 4:5).

Tertullian, A.D. 200 — "[T]he apostolic churches transmit their lists: like the church of the Smyrneans, which records that Polycarp was placed there by John, like the church of the Romans, where Clement was ordained by Peter" (*Demurrer Against the Heretics* 32:2).

St. Cyprian of Carthage, A.D. 251 — "The Lord says to Peter: 'I say to you,' he says, 'that you are Peter, and upon this rock I will build my Church, and the gates of hell will not overcome it.'[16] . . . On him he builds the Church, and to him he gives the command to feed the sheep,[17] and although he assigns a like power to all the apostles, yet he founded a single chair,[18] and he established by his own authority a source and an intrinsic reason for that unity. . . . If someone does not hold fast to this unity of Peter, can he imagine that he still holds the faith? If he [should] desert the chair of Peter upon whom the Church was built, can he still be confident that he is in the Church?" (*The Unity of the Catholic Church* 4).

St. Cyprian of Carthage, A.D. 253 — "[Pope] Cornelius was made bishop by the decision of God and of his Christ, by the testimony of almost all the clergy, by the applause of the people then present, by the college of venerable priests and good men, at a time when no one had been made [bishop] before him — when the place of [Pope] Fabian, which is the place of Peter, the dignity of the sacerdotal chair, was vacant. Since it has been occupied both at the will of

49

God and with the ratified consent of all of us, whoever now wishes to become bishop must do so outside. For he cannot have ecclesiastical rank who does not hold to the unity of the Church. . . . With a false bishop appointed for themselves by heretics, they dare even to set sail and carry letters from schismatics and blasphemers to the Chair of Peter and to the principal church [at Rome], in which sacerdotal unity has its source" (*Letter 55*, 8; 59:14).

Firmilian, A.D. 253 — "[Pope St.] Stephen . . . boasts of the place of his episcopate, and contends that he holds the succession from Peter, on whom the foundations of the Church were laid . . . [and] announces that he holds by succession the throne of Peter" (*Letter 74*, 17).

Eusebius of Caesarea, A.D. 312 — "Paul testifies that Crescens was sent to Gaul, but Linus, whom he mentions in the Second Epistle to Timothy[19] as his companion at Rome, was Peter's successor in the episcopate of the church there, as has already been shown. Clement also, who was appointed third bishop of the church at Rome, was, as Paul testifies, his co-laborer and fellow-soldier"[20] (*Ecclesiastical History* 3:4:9-10).

Pope Julius I, A.D. 341 — "Are you ignorant that the custom has been to write first to us [i.e., to the bishop of Rome] and then for a just decision to be passed from this place? If, then, any such suspicion rested upon the bishop there [Athanasius, bishop of Alexandria], notice of it ought to have been written to the church here. But now, after having done as they pleased, they want to obtain our concurrence, although we never condemned him. Not thus are the constitutions of Paul, not thus the traditions of the Fathers. This is another form of procedure, and a novel practice. . . . What I write about this is for the common good. For what we have heard from the blessed Apostle

Peter, these things I signify to you" (*Apology Against the Arians* 20-35).

The Council of Sardica, A.D. 342 — "[I]f any bishop loses the judgment in some case [decided by his fellow bishops] and still believes that he has not a bad but a good case, in order that the case may be judged anew . . . let us honor the memory of the Apostle Peter by having those who have given the judgment write to Julius, Bishop of Rome, so that if it seem proper he may himself send arbiters and the judgment may be made again by the bishops of a neighboring province" (canon 3).

The Council of Sardica — "If some bishop be deposed by the judgment of the bishops sitting in the neighborhood, and if he declare that he will seek further redress, another should not be appointed to his see until the Bishop of Rome can be acquainted with the case and render a judgment" (canon 4).

St. Epiphanius of Salamis, A.D. 375 — "At Rome the first Apostles and bishops were Peter and Paul, then Linus, then Cletus, then Clement, the contemporary of Peter and Paul" (*Medicine Chest Against All Heresies* 27:6).

St. Jerome, A.D. 396 — "Since the East, shattered as it is by the long-standing feuds, subsisting between its peoples, is bit by bit tearing into shreds the seamless vest of the Lord . . . I think it my duty to consult the chair of Peter, and to turn to a church [Rome] whose faith has been praised by Paul.[21] I appeal for spiritual food to the church whence I have received the garb of Christ. . . . Evil children have squandered their patrimony; you alone keep your heritage intact. . . . I follow no leader but Christ and join in communion with none but your blessedness [Pope Damasus I], that is, with the chair of Peter. I know that this is the rock on which the Church has been built. Whoever eats the Lamb outside this house is profane. Anyone who is not in the ark of Noah will perish when the flood prevails" (Letter 15, *To Pope Damasus* 1, 2).

St. Ambrose of Milan, A.D. 388 — "[The Novatianist heretics] have not the succession of Peter, who hold not the chair of Peter, which they rend by wicked schism; and this, too, they do, wickedly denying that sins can be forgiven even in the Church,[22] whereas it was said to Peter: 'I will give unto thee the keys of the kingdom of heaven. and whatsoever thou shalt bind on earth shall be bound also in heaven, and whatsoever thou shalt loose on earth shall be loosed also in heaven' " (*On Penance* 1:7:33).

St. Augustine of Hippo, A.D. 412 — "If the very order of episcopal succession is to be considered, how much more surely, truly, and safely do we number them from Peter himself, to whom, as to one representing the whole Church, the Lord said, 'Upon this rock I will build my church.'[23] . . . Peter was succeeded by Linus, Linus by Clement, Clement by Anacletus, Anacletus by Evaristus . . ." (Letter 53, *To Generosus* 1:2).

The Council of Ephesus, A.D. 431 — "Philip the presbyter and legate of the Apostolic See[24] said: 'There is no doubt, and in fact it has been known in all ages, that the holy and most blessed Peter, prince and head of the Apostles, pillar of the faith, and foundation of the Catholic Church, received the keys of the kingdom from our Lord Jesus Christ, the Savior and Redeemer of the human race, and that to him was given the power of loosing and binding sins: who down even to to-day and forever both lives and judges in his successors. The holy and most blessed pope Celestine, according to due order, is his successor and holds his place, and us he sent to supply his place in this holy synod' " (*Acts of the Council*, session 3).

Pope St. Leo the Great, A.D. 445 — "As for the resolution of the bishops which is contrary to the Nicene decree, in union with your faithful piety, I declare it to be invalid and annul it by the authority of the holy Apostle Peter" (Letter 105, *To Pulcheria Augusta*).

Pope St. Leo the Great, A.D. 450 — "[Christ said,] 'Blessed are you, Simon Bar-Jonah, because flesh and blood have not revealed it to you, but my Father, who is in heaven. And I say to you, that you are Peter, and upon this rock I will build my Church, and the gates of hell shall not prevail against it.' The dispensation of truth therefore abides, and the blessed Peter persevering in the strength of the rock, which he has received, has not abandoned the helm of the Church" (*Sermons* 3:2-3).

Pope St. Leo the Great, A.D. 449 — "Whereupon the blessed Peter, as inspired by God, and about to benefit all nations by his confession, said, 'You are the Christ, the Son of the living God.' Not undeservedly, therefore, was he pronounced blessed by the Lord, and derived from the original Rock that solidity which belonged both to his virtue and to his name"[25] (*The Tome of Leo*).

The Council of Chalcedon, A.D. 451 — "After the reading of the foregoing epistle,[26] the most reverend bishops cried out, 'This is the faith of the fathers! this is the faith of the Apostles! So we all believe! thus the orthodox believe! Anathema to him who does not thus believe! Peter has spoken thus through [Pope] Leo! . . . This is the true faith! Those of us who are orthodox thus believe! This is the faith of the Fathers!' " (*Acts of the Council*, session 2).

2. The Bishop of Rome Has Unique Authority

There are a vast number of examples from the early Church Fathers that we could use to demonstrate that the pope had a special primacy of authority in the Church, one that was readily recognized, even at times zealously defended, by bishops of other dioceses. One particularly striking example of an early bishop of Rome exercising this primacy of jurisdiction is in the reign of Pope Victor I. In the year 190, he labored to bring to an end the controversy between the East and Western Catholics over the question of when to celebrate Easter.[27]

Pope Victor threatened to excommunicate all the bishops of the East who did not submit to his decision on the matter. And while some bishops, such as St. Irenaeus of Lyons, complained about the pope's canonical threat, none of them denied or argued with the fact that the pope had the authority to do so.[28]

Consider these other examples of acknowledgment of the pope's primacy:

Pope St. Clement of Rome, circa A.D. 80 — "Owing to the sudden and repeated calamities and misfortunes which have befallen us, we must acknowledge that we have been somewhat tardy in turning our attention to the matters in dispute among you, beloved, and especially that abominable and unholy sedition, alien and foreign to the elect of God, which a few rash and self-willed persons have inflamed. Accept our counsel and you will have nothing to regret. . . . If anyone disobey the things which have been said by him [the Lord] through us, let them know that they will involve themselves in transgression and in no small danger. You will afford us joy and gladness if being obedient to the things which we have written through the Holy Spirit, you will root out the wicked passion of jealousy" (*Epistle to the Corinthians* 1:1, 58:2—59:1, 63:2).

Hermas, circa A.D. 80 — "Therefore shall you [Hermas] write two little books and send one to Clement [the bishop of Rome] and one to Grapte. Clement shall then send it to the cities abroad, because that is his duty" (*The Shepherd* 2:4:3).

St. Ignatius of Antioch, circa A.D. 107–110 — "Ignatius . . . to the church also which holds the presidency, in the location of the country of the Romans, worthy of God, worthy of honor, worthy of blessing, worthy of praise, worthy of success, worthy of sanctification, and, because you hold the presidency in love, named after Christ and named after the Father. . . . You [the Church at Rome] have envied no one, but others you have taught. I desire only that what you have enjoined in your instructions may remain in force" (*Letter to the Romans* 1:1).

St. Dionysius of Corinth, A.D. 170 — "For from the beginning it has been your custom to do good to all the brethren in various ways and to send contributions to all the churches in every city. . . . This custom your blessed Bishop Soter has not only preserved, but is augmenting, by furnishing an abundance of supplies to the saints and by urging with consoling words, as a loving father his children, the brethren who are journeying. . . . Today we have observed the Lord's holy day, in which we have read your letter. Whenever we do read it, we shall be able to profit thereby, as also we do when we read the earlier letter written to us by Clement" (*Epistle to Pope Soter,* quoted in Eusebius of Caesarea's *Ecclesiastical History* 4:23:9, 11).

St. Irenaeus of Lyons, A.D. 189 — "But since it would be too long to enumerate in such a volume as this the succession of all the churches, we shall confound all those who, in whatever manner, whether through self-satisfaction or vainglory, or through blindness and wicked opinion, assemble other than where it is proper, by pointing out here the successions of the bishops of the greatest and most ancient church known to all, founded and organized at Rome by the two most glorious apostles, Peter and Paul, that church which has the tradition and the faith which comes down to us after having been announced to men by the apostles. With that church, because of its superior origin, all the churches must agree, that is, all the faithful in the whole world, and it is in her that the faithful everywhere have maintained the apostolic tradition" (*Against Heresies* 3:3:2).

Tertullian, A.D. 220 — "I hear that there has even been an edict set forth, and a peremptory one too. The sovereign pontiff, that is the bishop of bishops, pronounces, 'I [Pope Callistus I] remit the crimes of adultery and fornications to those who have done penance.' . . . And to produce the aforesaid effect in a person, you [Pope Callistus I] make fine speeches with every possible allurement of pity [to those who have fallen] in the role of kind shepherd and blessed pope" (*On Modesty* 1, 13).

St. Cyprian of Carthage, A.D. 253 — "Cyprian to [Pope] Cornelius, his brother. Greeting. . . . We decided to send and are sending a letter to you from all throughout the province [where I am] so that all our colleagues might give their decided approval and support to you and to your communion, that is, to both the unity and the charity of the Catholic Church" (Letter 44, *To Cornelius* 1, 4).

St. Cyprian of Carthage — "Cyprian to Antonianus his brother, greeting. I received your first letters, dearest brother, firmly maintaining the concord of the priestly college, and adhering to the Catholic Church, in which you intimated that you did not hold communion with Novatian,[29] but followed my advice, and held one common agreement with [Pope] Cornelius our co-bishop. You wrote, moreover, for me to transmit a copy of those same letters to Cornelius our colleague, so that he might lay aside all anxiety, and know at once that you held communion with him, that is, with the Catholic Church" (Letter 51, *To Antonianus* 1).

3. The Bishop of Rome Is the Successor of Peter

Dionysius of Corinth, A.D. 170 — "You[30] have also, by your very admonition, brought together the planting that was made by Peter and Paul at Rome and at Corinth; for both of them alike planted in our Corinth and taught us; and both alike, teaching similarly in Italy, suffered martyrdom at the same time" (*Letter to Pope Soter*, quoted in Eusebius of Caesarea's *Ecclesiastical History* 2:25:8).

St. Irenaeus of Lyons, A.D. 189 — "Matthew also issued among the Hebrews a written Gospel in their own language, while Peter and Paul were evangelizing in Rome and laying the foundation of the Church. . . . But since it would be too long to enumerate in such a volume as this the succession of all the churches, we shall confound all those who, in whatever manner, whether through self-satisfaction or vainglory, or through blindness and wicked opinion, assemble other than where it is proper, by pointing out here the successions of the bishops of the greatest and most ancient church known to all, founded and organized at Rome by the two most glorious apostles, Peter and Paul, that church which has the tradition and the faith which comes down to us after having been announced to men by the apostles. With that church [i.e., with Rome], because of its superior origin, all the churches must agree, that is, all the faithful in the whole world, and it is in her that the faithful everywhere have maintained the apostolic tradition" (*Against Heresies* 3:1:1; 3:3:2).

St. Irenaeus of Lyons, A.D. 189 — "The blessed apostles [Peter and Paul], having founded and built up the church [of Rome], they handed over the office of the episcopate to Linus. Paul makes mention of this Linus in the letter to Timothy [2 Timothy 4:21]. To him succeeded Anacletus, and after him, in the third place from the apostles, Clement was chosen for the episcopate. He had seen the blessed apostles and was acquainted with them. It might be said that he still heard the echoes of the preaching of the apostles and had their traditions before his eyes. And not only he, for there were many still remaining who had been instructed by the apostles. In the time of Clement, no small dissension having arisen among the brethren in Corinth, the Church in Rome sent a very strong letter to the Corinthians, exhorting them to peace and renewing their faith. . . . To this Clement, Evaristus succeeded . . . and now, in the twelfth place after the apostles, the lot of the episcopate [of Rome] has fallen to Eleutherus. In this order, and by the teaching of the apostles handed down in the Church, the preaching of the truth has come down to us" (*Against Heresies* 3:3:3).

Caius,[31] **circa A.D. 198** — "It is recorded that Paul was beheaded in Rome itself, and Peter, likewise, was crucified, during the reign [of the Emperor Nero]. The account is confirmed by the names of Peter and Paul over the cemeteries there, which remain to the present time. And it is confirmed also by a stalwart man of the Church, Gaius by name, who lived in the time of Zephyrinus, bishop of Rome. This Gaius, in a written disputation with Proclus, the leader of the sect of Cataphrygians, says this of the places in which the remains of the aforementioned apostles were deposited: 'I can point out the trophies [i.e., the tombs] of the apostles. For if you are willing to go to the Vatican or to the Ostian Way, you will find the trophies of those who founded this Church' " (*Disputation with Proclus*, quoted in Eusebius of Caesarea's *Ecclesiastical History* 2:25:5).

St. Clement of Alexandria, A.D. 200 — "When Peter preached the Word publicly at Rome and declared the gospel by the Spirit, many who were present requested that Mark, who had been a long time his follower and who remembered his sayings, should write down what had been proclaimed" (quoted in Eusebius of Caesarea's *Ecclesiastical History* 6:14:1).

Tertullian, A.D. 210 — "But if you are near Italy, you have Rome, where authority is at hand for us too. What a happy church that is, on which the apostles poured out their whole doctrine with their blood; where Peter had a passion like that of the Lord, where Paul was crowned with the death of John [the Baptist, by being beheaded]" (*Demurrer Against the Heretics* 36).

Tertullian — "Let us see what milk the Corinthians drained from Paul; against what standard the Galatians were measured for correction; what the Philippians, Thessalonians, and Ephesians read; what even the nearby Romans sound forth, to whom both Peter and Paul bequeathed the gospel and even sealed it with their blood" (*Against Marcion* 4, 5:1).

Eusebius of Caesarea, A.D. 303 — "The Apostle Peter, after he has established the church in Antioch, is sent to Rome, where he remains as a bishop of that city, preaching the gospel for twenty-five years" (*The Chronicle*).

Lactantius, A.D. 318 — "When Nero was already reigning, Peter came to Rome, where, in virtue of the performance of certain miracles which he worked . . . he converted many to righteousness and established a firm and steadfast temple to God. When this fact was reported to Nero . . . he sprang to the task of tearing down the heavenly temple and of destroying righteousness. It was he that first persecuted the servants of God. Peter he fixed to a cross, and Paul he slew" (*The Deaths of the Persecutors* 2:5).

Optatus of Milevis, A.D. 367 — "You cannot deny that you are aware that in the city of Rome the episcopal chair was given first to Peter; the chair in which Peter sat, the same who was head — that is why he is also called *Cephas*[32] — of all the apostles; the one chair in which unity is maintained by all" (*The Schism of the Donatists* 2:2).

Pope St. Damasus I, A.D. 382 — "Likewise it is decreed: . . . [W]e have considered that it ought to be announced that although all the Catholic Churches spread abroad through the world comprise one bridal chamber of Christ, nevertheless, the holy Roman Church has been placed at the forefront not by the conciliar decisions of other churches, but has received the primacy by the evangelic voice of our Lord and Savior, who says, 'You are Peter, and upon this rock I will build my Church, and the gates of hell will not prevail against it; and I will give to you the keys of the kingdom of heaven, and whatever you shall have bound on earth will be bound in heaven, and whatever you shall have loosed on earth shall be loosed in heaven.'[33]

"The first see [i.e., diocese], therefore, is that of Peter the apostle, that of the Roman Church, which has neither stain nor blemish nor anything like it. The second see, however, is that at Alexandria, consecrated in behalf of blessed Peter by Mark, his disciple and an evangelist, who was sent to Egypt by the Apostle Peter, where he preached the word of truth and finished his glorious martyrdom. The third honorable see, indeed, is that at Antioch, which belonged to the most blessed Apostle Peter, where first he dwelt before he came to Rome and where the name *Christians* was first applied, as to a new people" (*Decree of Damasus* 3; emphasis mine).

St. Jerome, A.D. **383** — "Stephen [bishop of Rome]. . . was the blessed Peter's twenty-second successor in the See of Rome" (*Against the Luciferians* 23).

St. Augustine of Hippo, A.D. **402** — "If all men throughout the world were such as you most vainly accuse them of having been, what has the chair of the Roman church done to you, in which Peter sat, and in which Anastasius sits today?" (*Against the Letters of Petilanus* 2:118).

St. Peter Chrysologus, A.D. **449** — "We exhort you in every respect, honorable brother, to heed obediently what has been written by the most blessed pope of the city of Rome, for blessed Peter, who lives and presides in his own see, provides the truth of faith to those who seek it. For we, by reason of our pursuit of peace and faith, cannot try cases on the faith without the consent of the bishop of Rome" (Letter 25, *To Eutyches* 2).

4. The Authority of Apostolic Tradition

With all the evidences we have seen up to this point demonstrating the authenticity of Catholic Tradition — seeing how undeniably present it was in the early Church — we need not say much by way of explanation about what the early Church thought of the *authority* of Sacred Tradition. These few examples of patristic statements, drawn from across the first seven centuries of Christianity, are sufficient to prove that the earliest Christians regarded Sacred Tradition as authoritative and necessary. Tradition was, for the early Christians as it is now for modern-day Christians, the Church's way of ascertaining that her teachings were in conformity with what Christ and the Apostles taught. This was why, when a heresy such as Arianism sprang up, denying the Trinity and the divinity of Christ, the Church in the third and fourth centuries could adequately refute the scriptural claims of the Arians. Much like modern-day Jehovah's Witnesses or Mormons, the Arians could only quote Scripture (out of context and with erroneous interpretations, of course). They could not appeal to an unbroken Tradition of authentic interpretation of those Scripture passages. The Catholic Church could do so, though. And by her appeal to the authority of Apostolic Tradition, as a necessary compliment to Scripture, the Church was able to meet and defeat the doctrinal challenges raised by heresies such as Arianism, Nestorianism, the Monophysites, and other theologically aberrant groups.

Pope St. Clement I, circa A.D. 80 — "Then the reverence of the law is chanted, and the grace of the prophets is known, and the faith of the Gospels is established, and the Tradition of the Apostles is preserved, and the grace of the Church exults" (*Epistle to the Corinthians* 11).

St. Irenaeus of Lyons, A.D. 189 — "As I said before, the Church, having received this preaching and this faith, although she is disseminated throughout the whole world, yet guarded it, as if she occupied but one house. She likewise believes these things just as if she had but one soul and one and the same heart; and harmoniously she proclaims them and teaches them and hands them down, as if she possessed but one mouth. For, while the languages of the world are di-verse, nevertheless, the authority of the Tradition is one and the same. . . . That is why it is surely necessary to avoid them [i.e., those who deny Catholic teaching], while cherishing with the utmost diligence the things pertaining to the Church, and to lay hold of the Tradition of truth. . . . What if the Apostles had not in fact left writings to us? Would it not be necessary to follow the order of Tradition, which was handed down to those to whom they entrusted the Churches?" (*Against Heresies* 1:10:2; 3:4:1).

St. Irenaeus of Lyons — "It is possible, then, for everyone in every church, who may wish to know the truth, to contemplate the Tradition of the Apostles which has been made known throughout the whole world. And we are in a position to enumerate those who were instituted bishops by the Apostles and their successors to our own times — men who neither knew nor taught anything like these heretics rave about. But since it would be too long to enumerate in such a volume as this the successions of all the churches, we shall confound all those who, in whatever manner, whether through self-satisfaction or vainglory, or through blindness and wicked opinion, assemble other than where it is proper, by pointing out here the successions of the bishops of the greatest and most ancient church known to all, founded and organized at Rome by the two most glorious Apostles, Peter and Paul, that church which has the Tradition and the faith which comes down to us after having been announced to men by the Apostles. With this church, because of its superior origin, all churches must agree — that is, all the faithful in the whole world — and it is in her that the faithful everywhere have maintained the Apostolic Tradition" (*Against Heresies* 3:3:1-2).

St. Clement of Alexandria, A.D. 208 — "Well, they preserving the Tradition of the blessed doctrine derived directly from the holy Apostles, Peter, James, John, and Paul, the sons receiving it from the father (but few were like the fathers), came by God's will to us also to deposit those ancestral and apostolic seeds. And well I know that they will exult; I do not mean delighted with this tribute, but solely on account of the preservation of the truth, according as they delivered it. For such a sketch as this, will, I think, be agreeable to a soul desirous of preserving from loss the blessed Tradition" (*Miscellanies* 1:1).

Origen, A.D. 225 — "Although there are many who believe that they themselves hold to the teachings of Christ, there are yet some among them who think differently from their predecessors. The teaching of the Church has indeed been handed down through an order of succession from the Apostles and remains in the churches even to the present time. That alone is to be believed as the truth which is in no way at variance with ecclesiastical and Apostolic Tradition" (*The Fundamental Doctrines* 1:2).

St. Cyprian of Carthage, A.D. 253 — "The [Catholic] Church is one, and as she is one, cannot be both within and without. For if she is with Novatian [the heretic], she was not with [Pope] Cornelius. But if she was with Cornelius, who succeeded the bishop Fabian by lawful ordination, and whom, beside the honor of the priesthood, the Lord glorified also with martyrdom, Novatian is not in the Church; nor can he be reckoned as a bishop, who, succeeding to no one, and despising the evangelical and Apostolic Tradition, sprang from himself. For he who has not been ordained in the Church can neither have nor hold to the Church in any way" (Letter 75, *To Magnus on Baptizing the Novatians* 3).

Eusebius of Caesarea, A.D. 312 — "[Bishop] Papias,[34] who is now mentioned by us, affirms that he received the sayings of the Apostles from those who accompanied them, and he moreover asserts that he heard in person Aristion and the presbyter John. Accordingly he mentions them frequently by name, and in his writings gives their Traditions. . . . [There are] other passages of his in which he relates some miraculous deeds, stating that he acquired the knowledge of them from Tradition. . . . At that time[35] there flourished in the Church Hegesippus, whom we know from what has gone before, and Dionysius, bishop of Corinth, and another bishop, Pinytus of Crete, and besides these, Philip, and Apollinarius, and Melito, and Musanus, and Modestus, and finally, Irenaeus. From them has come down to us in writing, the sound and orthodox faith received from Tradition" (*Ecclesiastical History* 3:39; 4:21).

Eusebius of Caesarea — "A question of no small importance arose at that time.[36] For the parishes of all Asia . . . held that the fourteenth day of the moon, on which day the Jews were commanded to sacrifice the lamb, should be observed as the feast of the Savior's Passover. . . . But it was not the custom of the churches in the rest of the world to end it at this time, as they observed the practice which, from Apostolic Tradition, has prevailed to the present time, of terminating the [Lenten] fast on no other day than on that of the resurrection of our Savior [i.e., Sunday]" (*Ecclesiastical History* 4:23).

St. Athanasius of Alexandria, A.D. 330 — "Again we write, again keeping to the Apostolic Traditions, we remind each other when we come together for prayer; and keeping the feast in common, with one mouth we truly give thanks to the Lord. Thus giving thanks unto Him, and being followers of the saints, 'we shall make our praise in the Lord all the day,' as the Psalmist says. So, when we rightly keep the feast, we shall be counted worthy of that joy which is in heaven. . . . But you are blessed, who by faith are in the Church, dwell upon the foundations of the faith, and have full satisfaction, even the highest degree of faith which remains among you unshaken. For it has come down to you from Apostolic Tradition, and frequently accursed envy has wished to unsettle it, but has not been able" (*Festal Letters* 2:7, 29).

St. Basil the Great, A.D. **375** — "Of the dogmas and messages preserved in the Church, some we possess from written teaching and others we receive from the Tradition of the Apostles, handed on to us in mystery. In respect to piety both are of the same force. No one will contradict any of these, no one, at any rate, who is even moderately versed in matters ecclesiastical.[37] Indeed, were we to try to reject unwritten customs as having no great authority, we would unwittingly injure the gospel in its vitals; or rather, we would reduce the message [i.e., of the gospel] to a mere term" (*The Holy Spirit* 27:66).

St. Epiphanius of Salamis, A.D. **375** — "It is needful also to make use of Tradition, for not everything can be gotten from Sacred Scripture. The holy Apostles handed down some things in the Scriptures, other things in Tradition" (*Medicine Chest Against All Heresies* 61:6).

St. Augustine of Hippo, A.D. **400** — "The custom [of not rebaptizing heretics who reconcile with the Church] . . . may be supposed to have had its origin in Apostolic Tradition, just as there are many things which are observed by the whole Church, and therefore are fairly held to have been enjoined by the Apostles, which yet are not mentioned in their writings. . . . But the admonition that he [St. Cyprian of Carthage] gives us, 'that we should go back to the fountain, that is, to Apostolic Tradition, and thence turn the channel of truth to our times,' is most excellent, and should be followed without hesitation" (*On Baptism, Against the Donatists* 5:23, 26).

St. Augustine of Hippo — "But in regard to those observances which we carefully attend and which the whole world keeps, and which derive not from Scripture but from Tradition, we are given to understand that they are recommended and ordained to be kept, either by the Apostles themselves or by plenary [ecumenical] councils, the authority of which is quite vital in the Church" (*Epistle to Januarius*).

St. John Chrysostom, A.D. 402 — " 'Therefore, brethren, stand fast and hold the Traditions which you have been taught, whether by word or by our letter.' From this [quote from St. Paul; 2 Thessalonians 2:15] it is clear that they [the Apostles] did not hand down everything by letter, but there is much also that was not written. Like that which was written, the unwritten too is worthy of belief. So let us regard the Tradition of the Church also as worthy of belief. Is it a Tradition? Seek no further" (*Homilies on 2 Thessalonians*).

St. Vincent of Lerins, A.D. 434 — "With great zeal and closest attention, therefore, I frequently inquired of many men, eminent for their holiness and doctrine, how I might, in a concise and, so to speak, general and ordinary way, distinguish the truth of the Catholic faith from the falsehood of heretical depravity. I received almost always the same answer from all of them — that if I or anyone else wanted to expose the frauds and escape the snares of the heretics who rise up, and to remain intact and in sound faith, it would be necessary, with the help of the Lord, to fortify that faith in a twofold manner: first, of course, by the authority of divine law [i.e., Sacred Scripture] and then by the Tradition of the Catholic Church.

"Here, perhaps, someone may ask: 'If the canon of the Scriptures be perfect and in itself more than suffices for everything, why is it necessary that the authority of ecclesiastical interpretation be joined to it?' Because, quite plainly, Sacred Scripture, by reason of its own depth, is not accepted by everyone as having one and the same meaning. . . . Thus, because of so many distortions of such various errors, it is highly necessary that the line of prophetic and apostolic interpretation be directed in accord with the norm of the ecclesiastical and Catholic meaning" (*The Notebooks*).

Pope St. Agatho, A.D. 680 — "And briefly we shall intimate to [you], what the strength of our Apostolic Faith contains, which we have received through Apostolic Tradition and through the Tradition of the apostolical Pontiffs [i.e., the popes], and that of the five holy general synods [ecumenical councils], through which the foundations of Christ's Catholic Church have been strengthened and established. . . .

"For this is the rule of the true faith, which this spiritual mother of your most tranquil empire, the Apostolic Church of Christ, has both in prosperity and in adversity always held and defended with energy; which, it will be proved, by the grace of Almighty God, has never erred from the path of the Apostolic Tradition, nor has she been depraved by yielding to heretical innovations, but from the beginning she has received the Christian faith from her founders, the princes of the Apostles of Christ, and remains undefiled unto the end, according to the divine promise of the Lord and Savior himself" (*Epistle of Pope Agatho*, read at session IV of the Third Council of Constantinople).

Pope St. Agatho — "The Holy Church of God . . . has been established upon the firm rock of this Church of blessed Peter, the Prince of the Apostles, which by his grace and guardianship remains free from all error, the whole number of rulers and priests, of the clergy and of the people, unanimously should confess and preach with us as the true declaration of the Apostolic Tradition, in order to please God and to save their own souls" (*Epistle of Pope Agatho*, read at session IV of the Third Council of Constantinople).

---

5. The Canon of Scripture

The word "canon" comes from the Greek word *kanon*, which means a "measuring stick" or a defining rule. In the case of Scripture, its canon is the official list of inspired books that, taken together, make up what we know as the Bible. This official collection of seventy-three inspired books of the Old and New Testaments is itself part of God's revelation to the Church. He is the one who made these books inspired and, by virtue of that fact, canonical (cf. 2 Timothy 3:16) — not the Catholic Church. And this is a key issue in understanding the Tradition of the canon of Scripture. Many non-Catholics, especially Fundamentalist and Evangelical Protestants, argue against a caricature of the Catholic teaching by imagining, wrongly, that the Catholic Church claims that she herself made these books canonical. That is not true. The Catholic Church was the recipient of God's revelation about which books were inspired and which weren't. And because God revealed this truth, it is necessarily part of the Deposit of Faith, a Tradition that comes from God, not from men. It falls squarely into the realm of teaching that St. Paul said: "Stand firm and hold fast to the Traditions you were taught either by an oral statement or by a letter of ours" (2 Thessalonians 2:15).

All Protestants accept this crucial Catholic Tradition, though usually without realizing it is a Catholic Tradition, and they do so, ironically, while they at the same time condemn Catholic Tradition! Let's use the canon of the New Testament to illustrate this point. If you open a Protestant King James Version or New International Version (or some other) commonly used Protestant version of the Bible, you'll find the same twenty-seven books in that New Testament as you will find in any Catholic Bible — Matthew through Revelation. The same books in the same order. How did they get there?

The answer, of course, is that those Protestant Bibles rely completely on Catholic Tradition (though their editors would not likely acknowledge this) to know which books are in the New Testament. This Tradition of the canon of the New Testament was revealed by God, it was received and understood by the Church, it was eventually codified and made formal, and it was passed down in the Church for the last nineteen centuries through oral Tradition. Or, to put it another way, this Tradition that is so necessary for Christians to "stand firm and hold fast to" comes to us completely outside the pages of Scripture itself. Every Jehovah's Witness, Mormon, or Protestant "Bible Christian" you meet depends upon this vital Catholic Tradition, or he would not have a Bible. And that's the greatest irony of all: the non-Catholic who approaches you with Bible in hand, quoting Bible verses left and right in an attempt to disprove a given Catholic teaching, would not even have a Bible if not for the Catholic Church.

To summarize the Catholic Church's ancient Tradition on the canon of the Old and New Testaments, let's turn again to the *Catechism* for its official reiteration of Catholic teaching:

"It was by the apostolic Tradition that the Church discerned which writings are to be included in the list of the sacred books. This complete list is called the canon of Scripture. It includes 46 books for the Old Testament (45 if we count Jeremiah and Lamentations as one) and 27 for the New.

"*The Old Testament:* Genesis, Exodus, Leviticus, Numbers, Deuteronomy, Joshua, Judges, Ruth, 1 *and* 2 Samuel, 1 *and* 2 Kings, 1 *and* 2 Chronicles, Ezra *and* Nehemiah, Tobit, Judith, Esther, 1 *and* 2 Maccabees, Job, Psalms, Proverbs, Ecclesiastes, *the* Song of Songs, *the* Wisdom of Solomon, Sirach (Ecclesiasticus), Isaiah, Jeremiah, Lamentations, Baruch, Ezekiel, Daniel, Hosea, Joel, Amos, Obadiah, Jonah, Micah, Nahum, Habakkuk, Zephaniah, Haggai, Zechariah *and* Malachi.

"*The New Testament: the Gospels according to* Matthew, Mark, Luke *and* John, the Acts of the Apostles, *the* Letters of St. Paul to the Romans, 1 *and* 2 Corinthians, Galatians, Ephesians, Philippians, Colossians, 1 *and* 2 Thessalonians, 1 *and* 2 Timothy, Titus, Philemon, *the* Letter to the Hebrews, *the* Letters of James, 1 *and* 2 Peter, 1, 2, *and* John, *and* Jude, *and* Revelation (the Apocalypse)" (CCC 120).

The process of officially determining the extent of the canon was a long and painstaking one. We can see various examples of respected Church Fathers, such as St. Athanasius or St. Jerome, proposing canons that are slightly varied from the official version eventually settled on.[38] This should not disturb us because we should expect to find at least some differences of opinion on this issue during those years before the matter had been definitively settled by the Church. St. Athanasius, for example, championed a canon that was slightly different from the one we have today. St. Jerome, as an example, did not feel the Deuterocanonical books[39] should be considered part of the canon of the Old Testament, not because he disagreed with anything they contained, but because the Jews did not (by that point) include those books in their canon. But even the most brilliant biblical scholars should accept the authority of the magisterium, and it seems clear that St. Jerome did. Both Pope St. Damasus, in the year 382 at a synod in Rome, and Pope St. Innocent I, in a 405 letter to a bishop of Gaul answering his questions about the scope of the canon, taught that the canon of the Old Testament includes the Deuterocanonical books. What these popes taught was completely upheld by the North African councils of Carthage (A.D. 393, 397, 419) and Hippo (393), as well as by the Second Council of Nicaea (787), the Council of Florence (1434-1445), and the Council of Trent (1545-1563).

II. DOCTRINES

6. The Trinity

The belief in One God in Three Persons is one of Christianity's core defining doctrinal characteristics and underlies all else that is taught. This Tradition, founded on the Old Testament doctrine of monotheism (cf. Deuteronomy 6:4), was taught by Christ and the Apostles and was believed in the years preceding the Second Council of Nicaea, though it wasn't until that council, in the year 325, that the precise theological vocabulary we know today was developed by the magisterium.

It's amazing that the Catholic doctrine of the Blessed Trinity, one of the central doctrines of Christianity, is rejected by so many groups who claim to be "Christian." Modern-day groups such as the "Oneness Pentecostals," Jehovah's Witnesses, and Mormons reject the Church's teaching that there is One God in Three Divine Persons, the Father, the Son, and the Holy Spirit (cf. CCC 232-267).

But the Bible teaches, over against the errors of these groups, that there is One God, and that the Father is God, the Son is God, and the Holy Spirit is God. Since all Three are God and there is only One God, the Church teaches that the One True God has a Triune nature. The term developed for this reality is "The Trinity." The term "Trinity" seems to have been coined by Theophilus, the bishop of Antioch in A.D. 180, who said in his *Epistle to Autolycus*, a pagan critic of the Catholic Church:

> "And as the sun far surpasses the moon in power and glory, so far does God surpass man. And as the sun remains ever full, never becoming less, so does God always abide perfect, being full of all power, and understanding, and wisdom, and immortality,

and all good. But the moon wanes monthly, and in a manner dies, being a type of man; then it is born again, and is crescent, for a pattern of the future resurrection. In like manner also the three days which were before the luminaries, are types of the Trinity (Greek: *triados*), of God, and His Word [i.e., Christ], and His wisdom [i.e., the Holy Spirit]" (*To Autolycus* 2:15).

A few decades later, the great Latin exegete and theologian Tertullian (A.D. 160-circa 250)[40] used the term Trinity (Latin: *trinitas*) in his work *On Modesty*. He speaks of the "Trinity of the One Divinity; Father, Son, and Holy Spirit" (*On Modesty* 22).

By the fourth century, though, a roaring Christological heresy had swept across the Christian world like a prairie fire: Arianism. This heresy denied the Trinity and the concomitant doctrines of the divinity of Christ and of the Holy Spirit. The resulting turmoil caused by the Arian heresy was such that the Roman Emperor Constantine, determined to squash any religious upheaval that would threaten the well-being of the empire, called on all the Catholic bishops of the world to meet for a council to render binding judgment on the Arian position. This council is known as the First Council of Nicaea, held in A.D. 325.

The reason the threat posed by the Arians was so severe was that, on the theological level, their denial of the divinity of Christ struck at the heart of the Gospel. By declaring that Christ was not God but merely a superhuman creature, they in effect did away with the Incarnation and the Atonement and rendered the message of salvation void.

The assembled Catholic bishops, numbering some three hundred prelates from throughout the Catholic world, roundly condemned the Arian opinions denying Christ's divinity; they asserted the ancient Christian doctrine of One God in Three Persons; and they appealed as much to the authority of Sacred Tradition (i.e., the Church's lived understanding of the deposit of Faith given her by Christ and the Apostles) as they did to the authority of Scripture. In essence, the council rebuked the Arian heretics and overturned their efforts to be seen as legitimate Christians by asserting that their aberrant interpretations of Scripture about the nature of God could not be squared with the way in which the Catholic Church had always understood the meaning of those passages.[41] This appeal to Tradition effectively squelched the vitality of the Arian heresy, though it took many years before it finally ran out of steam and vanished.

Here are some examples of the early Church's statements on this fundamental Tradition of the Trinity:

Second Council of Nicaea, A.D. 325 — "We believe in one God, the Father Almighty, maker of all things visible and invisible; and in one Lord Jesus Christ, the Son of God, the only-begotten of his Father, of the substance of the Father, God of God, Light of Light, very God of very God, begotten, not made, being of one substance (Greek: *homoousion*, Latin: *consubstantialem*) with the Father. By whom all things were made, both which be in heaven and in earth. Who for us men and for our salvation came down [from heaven] and was incarnate and was made *man*. He suffered and the third day he rose again, and ascended into heaven. And he shall come again to judge both the quick and the dead. And [we believe] in the Holy Ghost. And whosoever shall say that there was a time when the Son of God was not (Greek: *en pote hote ouk en*), or that before he was begotten he was not, or that he was made of things that were not, or that he is of a different substance or essence [from the

Father] or that he is a creature, or subject to change or conversion — all that so say, the Catholic and Apostolic Church anathematizes them" (The Creed).

The *Didache*, A.D. 70 — "After the foregoing instructions, baptize in the name of the Father, and of the Son, and of the Holy Spirit, in living water. . . . If you have neither, pour water three times on the head, in the name of the Father, and of the Son, and of the Holy Spirit" (7:1).

Ignatius of Antioch, circa A.D. 107–110 — "[T]o the Church at Ephesus in Asia . . . chosen through true suffering by the will of the Father in Jesus Christ our God. . . . For our God, Jesus Christ, was conceived by Mary in accord with God's plan: of the seed of David, it is true, but also of the Holy Spirit" (*Epistle to the Ephesians* 1:1; 18:2).

Justin Martyr, A.D. 151 — "We will prove that we worship him reasonably; for we have learned that he is the Son of the true God Himself, that he holds a second place, and the Spirit of prophecy a third. For this they accuse us of madness, saying that we attribute to a crucified man a place second to the unchangeable and eternal God, the Creator of all things; but they are ignorant of the Mystery which lies therein" (*First Apology* 13:5-6).

Athenagoras, circa A.D. 177 — "The Son of God is the Word of the Father in thought and actuality. By him and through him all things were made, the Father and the Son being one. Since the Son is in the Father and the Father is in the Son by the unity and power of the Spirit, the Mind and Word of the Father is the Son of God. And if, in your exceedingly great wisdom, it occurs to you to inquire what is meant by 'the Son,' I will tell you briefly: He is the first-begotten of the Father, not as having been produced, for from the beginning God had the Word in himself,

God being eternal mind and eternally rational, but as coming forth to be the model and energizing force of all material things" (*Plea for the Christians* 10:2-4).

St. Irenaeus of Lyons, A.D. 189 — "For the Church, although dispersed throughout the whole world even to the ends of the earth, has received from the Apostles and from their disciples the faith in one God, the Father Almighty . . . and in one Jesus Christ, the Son of God, who became flesh for our salvation; and in the Holy Spirit" (*Against Heresies* 1:10:1).

Pope St. Dionysius, A.D. 262 — "Therefore, the divine Trinity must be gathered up and brought together in one, a summit, as it were, I mean the omnipotent God of the universe. . . . It is blasphemy, then, and not a common one but the worst, to say that the Son is in any way a handiwork [i.e., merely a creature]. . . . But if the Son came into being, [then] there was a time when these attributes did not exist; and, consequently, there was a time when God was without them, which is utterly absurd. . . . Neither, then, may we divide into three godheads the wonderful and divine unity. . . . Rather, we must believe in God, the Father almighty; and in Christ Jesus, his Son; and in the Holy Spirit; and that the Word is united to the God of the Universe. 'For,' he says, 'the Father and I are one,' and 'I am in the Father, and the Father in me' " (*Letter to Dionysius of Alexandria* 1, 2).

St. Gregory Thaumaturges, A.D. 265 — "There is one God. . . . There is a perfect Trinity, in glory and eternity and sovereignty, neither divided nor estranged. Wherefore there is nothing either created or in servitude in the Trinity; nor anything superinduced, as if at some former period it was non-existent, and at some later period it was introduced. And thus neither was the Son ever wanting to the Father, nor the Spirit to the Son; but without variation and without change, the same Trinity abides ever" (*Declaration of Faith*).

7. Mary as the Mother of God and Her Perpetual Virginity

The two Catholic Traditions of Mary's perpetual virginity and that she is the Mother of God (Greek: *Theotokos* = "God-bearer") are hotly disputed by many non-Catholics.

Against the first doctrine, they argue that Mary could not have remained a virgin for the rest of her life because the Bible speaks of "brothers of the Lord" in several instances. This, they believe, shows that Mary and Joseph must have engaged in sexual relations at some point after the birth of Christ in order that his "brothers" would be born. But the Catholic Church, since the time of the first century, has rejected such a view. The Catholic Church teaches that Mary remained a virgin her entire life.

Against the second doctrine, that she is the Mother of God, they argue that she couldn't be God's mother because that would entail that she preexisted God, which would be absurd. The Catholic Church agrees that such a notion is absurd, but by hailing Mary as the "Mother of God," the Church does not in any way teach or imply that she preexisted God. Rather, very early on, the Catholic Church recognized that the title "Mother of God" (derived from the Greek term *Theotokos*, "God bearer") is the most accurate way of describing her maternal relationship with Jesus.[42] This is because she didn't give birth simply to Christ's human nature, as many who oppose this doctrine will argue. No, she gave birth, as all human mothers do, to a *person*. No new mother speaks about the newborn baby she cradles in her arms as the "nature" that was born to her. She speaks of the "person" who was born. And the same is true of Mary and Jesus. As the Council of Chalcedon defined, in Christ there is only one person, the Second Person of the Blessed Trinity. At the Incarnation he took on human nature, but he was not a human person, but God Himself. So this is why the Catholic Church has always pointed to the truth that the Blessed Virgin Mary was truly the Mother of God, for it was God himself who was born from her womb, some twenty centuries ago, in that stable in Bethlehem.

St. Elizabeth proclaimed this great truth about Mary as the Mother of God when she exclaimed, "Who am I that *the mother of my Lord* should come to me?" (Luke 1:43; emphasis mine).

One early example of the Church affirming these two Marian doctrines came in A.D. 392, when Pope St. Siricius (384–398) declared in a letter to the bishop of Thessalonica the Church's certainty of Mary's perpetual virginity.[43] But there are many other and much earlier examples of such affirmations. Here are a few of them:

St. Irenaeus of Lyons, A.D. 189 — "The Virgin Mary, being obedient to his word, received from an angel the glad tidings that she would bear God" (*Against Heresies*, 5:19:1).

St. Irenaeus of Lyons — "Consequently, then, Mary the Virgin is found to be obedient, saying, 'Behold, O Lord, your handmaid; be it done to me according to your word.' Eve, however, was disobedient, and, when yet a virgin, she did not obey. Just as she, who was then still a virgin although she had Adam for a husband — for in paradise they were both naked but were not ashamed; for, having been created only a short time, they had no understanding of the procreation of children, and it was necessary that they first come to maturity before beginning to multiply — having become disobedient, was made the cause of death for herself and for the whole human race; so also Mary, betrothed to a man but nevertheless still a virgin, being obedient, was made the cause of salvation for herself and for the whole human race. Thus, the knot of Eve's disobedience was loosed by the obedience of Mary. What the virgin Eve had bound in unbelief, the Virgin Mary loosed through [her] faith" (*Against Heresies* 3:22:24).

Tertullian, A.D. 210 — "And again, lest I depart from my argumentation on the name of Adam: Why is Christ called Adam by the apostle, if as man he was not of that earthly origin? But even reason defends this conclusion, that God recovered his image and likeness by a procedure similar to that in which he had been robbed of it by the devil. It was while Eve was still a virgin that the word of the devil crept in to erect an edifice of death. Likewise through a Virgin the Word of God was introduced to set up a structure of life. Thus what had been laid waste in ruin by this sex was by the same sex re-established in salvation. Eve had believed the serpent; Mary believed Gabriel. That which the one destroyed by believing, the other, by believing, set straight" (*The Flesh of Christ* 17:4).

St. Hippolytus, A.D. 217 — "[T]o all generations they [the prophets] have pictured forth the grandest subjects for contemplation and for action. Thus, too, they preached of the advent of God in the flesh to the world, His advent by the spotless and God-bearing (Greek: *Theotokos*) Mary in the way of birth and growth, and the manner of His life and conversation with men, and His manifestation by baptism, and the new birth that was to be to all men, and the regeneration by the laver [of baptism]" (*Discourse on the End of the World* 1).

St. Gregory Thaumaturges, A.D. 262 — "For Luke, in the inspired Gospel narratives, delivers a testimony not to Joseph only, but also to Mary the Mother of God, and gives this account with reference to the very family and house of David" (*Four Homilies* 1).

St. Gregory Thaumaturges — "It is our duty to present to God, like sacrifices, all the festivals and hymnal celebrations; and first of all, [the feast of] the Annunciation to the holy Mother of God, to wit, the salutation made to her by the angel, 'Hail, full of grace!' " (*Four Homilies* 2).

Peter of Alexandria, A.D. 305 — "[T]hey came to the church of the most blessed Mother of God, and Ever-Virgin Mary, which, as we began to say, he had constructed in the western quarter, in a suburb, for a cemetery of the martyrs" (*The Genuine Acts of Peter of Alexandria*).

St. Methodius, A.D. 305 — "While the old man [Simeon] was thus exultant, and rejoicing with exceeding great and holy joy, that which had before been spoken of in a figure by the prophet Isaiah, the holy Mother of God now manifestly fulfilled" (*Oration on Simeon and Anna* 7).

St. Methodius — "Hail to thee for ever, you virgin Mother of God, our unceasing joy, for unto thee do I again return. . . . Hail, you fount of the Son's love for man. . . . Wherefore, we pray thee, the most excellent among women, who boasts in the confidence of your maternal honors, that you would unceasingly keep us in remembrance. O holy Mother of God, remember us, I say, who make our boast in thee, and who in hymns august celebrate the memory, which will ever live, and never fade away" (*Oration on Simeon and Anna* 14).

St. Alexander of Alexandria, A.D. 324 — "We acknowledge the resurrection of the dead, of which Jesus Christ our Lord became the firstling; he bore a body not in appearance but in truth derived from Mary the Mother of God" (*Letter to All Non-Egyptian Bishops* 12).

St. Cyril of Jerusalem, A.D. 350 — "The Father bears witness from heaven to his Son. The Holy Spirit bears witness, coming down bodily in the form of a dove. The Archangel Gabriel bears witness, bringing the good tidings to Mary. The Virgin Mother of God bears witness" (*Catechetical Lectures* 10:19).

St. Ephraim the Syrian, A.D. 351 — "Though still a virgin she carried a child in her womb, and the handmaid and work of his wisdom became the Mother of God" (*Songs of Praise* 1:20).

St. Athanasius, A.D. 365 — "The Word begotten of the Father from on high, inexpressibly, inexplicably, incomprehensibly, and eternally, is he that is born in time here below of the Virgin Mary, the Mother of God" (*The Incarnation of the Word of God* 8).

St. Epiphanius of Salamis, A.D. 374 — "Being perfect at the side of the Father and incarnate among us, not in appearance but in truth, he [Christ] reshaped man to perfection in himself from Mary the Mother of God through the Holy Spirit" (*The Man Well-Anchored* 75).

St. Ambrose of Milan, A.D. 377 — "The first thing which kindles ardor in learning is the greatness of the teacher. What is greater than the Mother of God? What more glorious than she whom glory itself chose?" (*The Virgins* 2:2).

St. Gregory Nazianzen, A.D. 382 — "If anyone does not agree that Holy Mary is Mother of God, he is at odds with the Godhead" (*Letter to Cledonius the Priest* 101).

St. Jerome, A.D. 401 — "As to how a virgin became the Mother of God, he [Rufinus] has full knowledge; as to how he himself was born, he knows nothing" (*Against Rufinus* 2:10).

St. Jerome, A.D. 409 — "Do not marvel at the novelty of the thing, if a Virgin gives birth to God" (*Commentaries on Isaiah* 3:7:15).

Theodore of Mopsuestia, A.D. 405 — "When, therefore, they ask, 'Is Mary mother of man or Mother of God?' we answer, 'Both!' The one by the very nature of what was done and the other by relation. Mother of man because it was a man who was in the womb of Mary and who came forth from there, and the Mother of God because God was in the man who was born" (*The Incarnation* 15).

St. Cyril of Alexandria, A.D. 427 — "I have been amazed that some are utterly in doubt as to whether or not the Holy Virgin is able to be called the Mother of God. For if our Lord Jesus Christ is God, how should the Holy Virgin who bore him not be the Mother of God?" (*Letter to the Monks of Egypt* 1).

St. Cyril of Alexandria, A.D. 430 — "This expression, however, 'the Word was made flesh,'[44] can mean nothing else but that he partook of flesh and blood like to us; he made our body his own, and came forth man from a woman, not casting off his existence as God, or his generation of God the Father, but even in taking to himself flesh remaining what he was. This the declaration of the correct faith proclaims everywhere. This was the sentiment of the holy Fathers; therefore they ventured to call the holy Virgin, the Mother of God, not as if the nature of the Word or his divinity had its beginning from the holy Virgin, but because of her was born that holy body with a rational soul, to which the Word, being personally united, is said to be born according to the flesh" (*First Letter to Nestorius*).

St. Cyril of Alexandria, A.D. 430 — "And since the holy Virgin corporally brought forth God made one with flesh according to nature, for this reason we also call her Mother of God, not as if the nature of the Word had the beginning of its existence from the flesh. . . . If anyone will not confess that the Emmanuel is very God, and that therefore the Holy Virgin is the Mother of God, inasmuch as in the flesh she bore the Word of God made flesh,[45] let him be anathema" (*Third Letter to Nestorius*).

St. John Cassian, A.D. 429 — "Now, you heretic, you say (whoever you are who deny that God was born of the Virgin), that Mary, the Mother of our Lord Jesus Christ, cannot be called the Mother of God, but the Mother only of Christ and not of God, for no one, you say, gives birth to one older than herself. And concerning this utterly stupid argument . . . let us prove by divine testimonies both that Christ is God and that Mary is the Mother of God. . . . You cannot then help admitting that the grace comes from God. It is God then who has given it. But it has been given by our Lord Jesus Christ. Therefore the Lord Jesus Christ is God. But if He is God, as he certainly is, then she who bore God is the Mother of God" (*On the Incarnation of Christ Against Nestorius* 2:2, 5).

The Council of Ephesus, A.D. 431 — "We confess, then, our Lord Jesus Christ, the only begotten Son of God perfect God and perfect man of a rational soul and a body, begotten before all ages from the Father in his godhead, the same in the last days, for us and for our salvation, born of Mary the virgin, according to his humanity, one and the same consubstantial with the Father in godhead and consubstantial with us in humanity, for a union of two natures took place. Therefore we confess one Christ, one Son, one Lord. According to this understanding of the unconfused union, we confess the holy virgin to be the Mother of God because God the Word took flesh and became man and from his very conception united to himself the temple he took from her" (*Formula of Union*).

Vincent of Lerins, A.D. 434 — "Nestorius, whose disease is of an opposite kind, while pretending that he holds two distinct substances in Christ, brings in of a sudden two Persons, and with unheard of wickedness would have two sons of God, two Christs, — one, God, the other, man; one, begotten of his Father, the other, born of his mother. For which reason he maintains that Saint Mary ought to be called, not the Mother of God, but the mother of Christ" (*The Notebooks* 12).

The Council of Chalcedon, A.D. 451 — "So, *following the saintly fathers*, we all with one voice teach the confession of one and the same Son, our Lord Jesus Christ: the same perfect in divinity and perfect in humanity, the same truly God and truly man, of a rational soul and a body; consubstantial with the Father as regards his divinity, and the same consubstantial with us as regards his humanity; like us in all respects except for sin; begotten before the ages from the Father as regards his divinity, and in the last days the same for us and for our salvation *from Mary, the virgin God-bearer* as regards his humanity; one and the same Christ, Son, Lord, only-begotten, acknowledged in two natures which undergo no confusion, no change, no division, no separation; at no point was the difference between the natures taken away through the union, but rather the property of both natures is preserved and comes together into a single person and a single subsistent being; he is not parted or divided into two persons, but is one and the same only-begotten Son, God, Word, Lord Jesus Christ, just as the prophets taught from the beginning about him, and as the Lord Jesus Christ himself instructed us, and as the creed of the fathers handed it down to us" (*The Confession of Faith*, Council of Chalcedon; emphasis mine).

St. Gregory of Tours, A.D. 584 — "But Mary, the glorious Mother of Christ, who is believed to be a virgin both before and after she bore him, has, as we said above, been translated into paradise, amid the singing of the angelic choirs, whither the Lord preceded her" (*Eight Books of Miracles* 1:4, 8).

8. Honoring Mary and the Saints and Praying to Them

The Tradition of the communion of saints — that is, the doctrine that all Christians who are in the state of grace, whether on earth, in heaven, or in purgatory — gave rise to various "small-t" traditions in the early Church that showed forth the meaning of this doctrine. Among the many practices we see very early in the Church are the veneration of the relics of the martyrs, the remembrance of the martyrs and deceased holy Christians during the Eucharistic sacrifice, and in due time, a broader application of veneration to the saints (i.e., including non-martyrs) in general. Among all the various Christian customs pertaining to the communion of saints that sprang up over the centuries, the Blessed Virgin Mary has a prominent role. Her role as Mother of the Church, Mother of God, Bride the Holy Spirit, and the New Eve (Mother of the Redeemed Human Race) finds expression in the Church's traditional hymns, artwork, and in the theological writings of the Fathers and Doctors.

Protestant historian J.N.D. Kelly comments on this development:

"A phenomenon of great significance in the patristic period (i.e., during the time of the Fathers of the Church; from the apostolic era to, roughly, the eighth century) was the rise and gradual development of veneration for the saints, more particularly for the Blessed Virgin Mary. . . . The earliest in the field was the cult[46] of martyrs, the heroes of the Faith whom Christians held to be already in God's presence and glorious in his sight (cf. Pope St. Clement of Rome's *Epistle to the Corinthians* 5:4). At first it took the form of reverent preservation of their relics and the annual celebration of their 'birthdays' (i.e., the date of their martyrdoms on which they were reborn into eternal life). From this it was a short step, since they (the Martyrs) were now with Christ in glory, to seeking their help and prayers. . . ."[47]

This Tradition of honoring the saints and asking for their intercession manifested itself in the Church's liturgies, artwork, prayers, feast day celebrations, etc. None of these things were (or are) intended in any way to sidetrack a Christian from his duty to know, love, and serve God with all his heart and soul. Rather, the ancient Christian practice of honoring Mary and the saints was a further way for the Church to rejoice in God's blessings and to glorify God all the more by honoring his grace in the lives of those who were faithful and heroic witnesses for Christ.

When we see a beautiful sunset or a breathtakingly beautiful mountain, we can praise its natural beauty and in so doing, we are praising God its creator. Praising the beauty of God's creations is another form of rendering praise to God himself. It never competes with our worship of God alone. Rather, it completes it.

Consider the evidence for this Tradition of honoring the saints and asking them for their prayerful intercession drawn from these early Christian writers:

St. Clement of Alexandria, A.D. 208 — "In this way is he always pure for prayer. He also prays in the society of angels, as being already of angelic rank, and he is never out of their holy keeping; and though he pray alone, he has the choir of the saints standing with him [in prayer]" (*Miscellanies* 7:12).

Origen, A.D. 233 — "But not [Jesus] the high priest alone prays for those who pray sincerely, but also the angels . . . as also the souls of the saints who have already fallen asleep [i.e., died]" (*On Prayer* 11).

St. Cyprian of Carthage, A.D. 235 — "Let us remember one another in concord and unanimity. Let us on both sides always pray for one another. Let us relieve burdens and afflictions by mutual love, that if one of us, by the swiftness of divine condescension, shall go hence the first, our love may continue in the presence of the Lord, and our prayers for our brethren and sisters not cease in the presence of the Father's mercy" (*Epistle* 56:5).

St. Cyril of Jerusalem, A.D. 350 — "[At the Offertory of the Liturgy of the Eucharist] we make mention also of those who have already fallen asleep [i.e., died]: first, the patriarchs, prophets, apostles, and martyrs, that through their prayers and supplications God would receive our petition" (*Catechetical Lectures* 23:9).

Hilary of Poitiers, A.D. 365 — "To those who wish to stand [in God's grace], neither the guardianship of saints nor the defenses of angels are wanting" (*Commentary on the Psalms* 124:5:6).

St. Ephraim the Syrian, A.D. 370 — "Remember me, you heirs of God, you brethren of Christ; supplicate the Savior earnestly for me, that I may be freed through Christ from him that fights against me day by day" (*The Fear at the End of Life*).

St. Ephraim the Syrian, A.D. 370 — "You victorious martyrs who endured torments gladly for the sake of the God and Savior, you who have boldness of speech toward the Lord himself, you saints, intercede for us who are timid and sinful men, full of sloth, that the grace of Christ may come upon us, and enlighten the hearts of all of us that we may love him" (*Commentary on Mark*).

St. Basil the Great, A.D. 373 — "By the command of your only-begotten Son we communicate with the memory of your saints . . . by whose prayers and supplications have mercy upon us all, and deliver us for the sake of your holy name" (*Liturgy of St. Basil*).

---

9. Purgatory and Prayers for the Deceased

This issue is a major stumbling block for many non-Catholics, especially Protestants and Jehovah's Witnesses. The Catholic traditions of purgatory (a temporary state or process of purification, carried out by God's fiery love on the soul of a man who dies in the state of grace and is destined for heaven) and praying for the repose of the souls in purgatory (praying for the deceased) have their foundation in the doctrine of the communion of saints. A common Catholic prayer that stems from this Tradition is "May the souls of the faithful departed rest in peace. Amen." This wonderfully compact prayer expresses very well the solidarity we have in Christ with all members of his body, including those who suffer in purgatory. To explain this Tradition to non-Catholics, follow these three steps in the explanation:

First, the doctrine of purgatory was not "invented" by Catholics in the eleventh or twelfth century, as some Protestants and others erroneously assume. This ancient Christian teaching, that there is a process of purification that the souls of some of those who die in the state of friendship with God (cf. Romans 11:22) will undergo, is well attested to by St. Paul in his teaching in 1 Corinthians 3:10-15.[48]

Second, anyone who goes through this process of purification that we call purgatory remains in the Body of Christ. In other words, there is only one Body of Christ, and all members of it — whether they be in heaven, in purgatory, or on earth — are intimately united to Christ and, through Christ, to every other member of the Body (cf. 1 Corinthians 12:12-27). This glorious and all-encompassing permanent connection that all Christians (i.e., members of the Mystical Body of Christ[49]) share with one another is the result of each member being united to Christ. As He said, "I am the vine, you are the branches" (John 15:5). Because we are united with Christ, we are united with every other person who is united with Christ (cf. 1 Corinthians 12:12-13, 20-21).

And third, when Christians on earth (as well as those in heaven) pray for the souls in purgatory, it is one way in which we live out our commandment from the Lord to "love one another" (cf. John 13:34, 15:12; Romans 13:8). As St. Paul emphasizes: "Bear one another's burdens, and so you will fulfill the law of Christ" (Galatians 6:2, NAB). The early Church clearly understood the Apostles' teaching on purgatory. Take a look:

Tertullian, A.D. 211 — "We offer sacrifices for the dead[50] on their birthday anniversaries" (*The Crown* 3:3).

Tertullian, A.D. 216 — "A woman, after the death of her husband . . . prays for his soul and asks that he may, while waiting, find rest; and that he may share in the first resurrection. And each year, on the anniversary of his death, she offers the sacrifice" (*On Monogamy* 10:1–2).

St. Cyprian of Carthage, A.D. **253** — "The strength of the truly believing remains unshaken; and with those who fear and love God with their whole heart, their integrity continues steady and strong. For to adulterers even a time of repentance is granted by us, and peace is given. Yet virginity is not therefore deficient in the Church, nor does the glorious design of continence languish through the sins of others. The Church, crowned with so many virgins, flourishes; and chastity and modesty preserve the tenor of their glory. Nor is the vigor of continence broken down because repentance and pardon are facilitated to the adulterer. It is one thing to stand for pardon, another thing to attain to glory; it is one thing, when cast into prison, not to go out thence until one has paid the uttermost farthing; another thing at once to receive the wages of faith and courage. It is one thing, tortured by long suffering for sins, to be cleansed and long purged by fire; another to have purged all sins by suffering. It is one thing, in fine, to be in suspense till the sentence of God at the day of judgment; another to be at once crowned by the Lord" (Letter 51, *To Antonianus* 20).

Lactantius, A.D. **307** — "But also, when God will judge the just, it is likewise in fire that he will try them. At that time, they whose sins are uppermost, either because of their gravity or their number, will be drawn together by the fire and will be burned. Those, however, who have been imbued with full justice and maturity of virtue, will not feel that fire; for they have something of God in them which will repel and turn back the strength of the flame" (*Divine Institutes* 7:21:6).

St. Cyril of Jerusalem, A.D. **350** — "Then we make mention also of those who have already fallen asleep: first, the patriarchs, prophets, apostles, and martyrs, that through their prayers and supplications God would receive our petition; next, we make mention also of the holy fathers and bishops who have already fallen asleep, and, to put it simply, of all among us who have already fallen asleep, for we believe that it will be of very great benefit to the souls of those for whom the petition is carried up, while this holy and most solemn sacrifice is laid out" (*Catechetical Lectures* 23:5:9).

St. Epiphanius of Salamis, A.D. **375** — "Useful too is the prayer fashioned on their behalf, even if it does not force back the whole of guilty charges laid to them. And it is useful also, because in this world we often stumble either voluntarily or involuntarily, and thus it is a reminder to do better" (*Medicine Chest Against All Heresies* 75:8).

St. Gregory of Nyssa, A.D. **382** — "If a man distinguish in himself what is peculiarly human from that which is irrational, and if he be on the watch for a life of greater urbanity for himself, in this present life he will purify himself of any evil contracted, overcoming the irrational by reason. If he have inclined to the irrational pressure of the passions, using for the passions the cooperating hide of things irrational, he may afterward in a quite different manner be very much interested in what is better, when, after his departure out of the body, he gains knowledge of the difference between virtue and vice and finds that he is not able to partake of divinity until he has been purged of the filthy contagion in his soul by the purifying fire" (*Sermon on the Dead*).

St. John Chrysostom, A.D. **392** — "Let us help and commemorate them. If Job's sons were purified by their father's sacrifice,[51] why would we doubt that our offerings for the dead bring them some consolation? Let us not hesitate to help those who have died and to offer our prayers for them" (*Homilies on 1 Corinthians* 41:5).

St. John Chrysostom, A.D. 402 — "Weep for those who die in their wealth and who with all their wealth prepared no consolation for their own souls, who had the power to wash away their sins and did not will to do it. Let us weep for them, let us assist them to the extent of our ability, let us think of some assistance for them, small as it may be, yet let us somehow assist them. But how, and in what way? By praying for them and by entreating others to pray for them, by constantly giving alms to the poor on their behalf. Not in vain was it decreed by the apostles that in the awesome mysteries remembrance should be made of the departed. They knew that here there was much gain for them, much benefit. When the entire people stands with hands uplifted, a priestly assembly, and that awesome sacrificial Victim is laid out, how, when we are calling upon God, should we not succeed in their defense? But this is done for those who have departed in the faith, while even the catechumens are not reckoned as worthy of this consolation, but are deprived of every means of assistance except one. And what is that? We may give alms to the poor on their behalf" (*Third Homily on Philippians*).

St. Augustine of Hippo, A.D. 411 — "There is an ecclesiastical discipline, as the faithful know, when the names of the martyrs are read aloud in that place at the altar of God, where prayer is not offered for them. Prayer, however, is offered for other dead who are remembered. It is wrong to pray for a martyr, to whose prayers we ought ourselves be commended" (*Sermons* 159:1).

St. Augustine of Hippo — "But by the prayers of the Holy Church, and by the salvific sacrifice, and by the alms which are given for their spirits, there is no doubt that the dead are aided, that the Lord might deal more mercifully with them than their sins would deserve. The whole Church observes this practice which was handed down by the Fathers: that it prays for those who have died in the communion of the Body and Blood of Christ, when they are commemorated in their own place in the sacrifice itself; and the sacrifice is offered also in memory of them, on their behalf. If, then, works of mercy are celebrated for the sake of those who are being remembered, who would hesitate to recommend them, on whose behalf prayers to God are not offered in vain? It is not at all to be doubted that such prayers are of profit to the dead; but for such of them as lived before their death in a way that makes it possible for these things to be useful to them after death" (*Sermons* 172:2).

St. Augustine of Hippo, A.D. **419** — "Temporal punishments are suffered by some in this life only, by some after death, by some both here and hereafter, but all of them before that last and strictest judgment. But not all who suffer temporal punishments after death will come to eternal punishments, which are to follow after that judgment. . . . The prayer either of the Church herself or of pious individuals is heard on behalf of certain of the dead, but it is heard for those who, having been regenerated in Christ, did not for the rest of their life in the body do such wickedness that they might be judged unworthy of such mercy,[52] nor who yet lived so well that it might be supposed they have no need of such mercy" (*The City of God* 21:13).

St. Augustine of Hippo, A.D. **421** — "That there should be some fire even after this life is not incredible, and it can be inquired into and either be discovered or left hidden whether some of the faithful may be saved, some more slowly and some more quickly in the greater or lesser degree in which they loved the good things that perish, through a certain purgatorial fire" (*Handbook on Faith, Hope, and Charity* 18:69).

St. Augustine of Hippo — "The time which interposes between the death of a man and the final resurrection holds souls in hidden retreats, accordingly as each is deserving of rest or of hardship, in view of what it merited when it was living in the flesh. Nor can it be denied that the souls of the dead find relief through the piety of their friends and relatives who are still alive, when the Sacrifice of the Mediator[53] is offered for them, or when alms are given in the Church. But these things are of profit to those who, when they were alive, merited that they might afterward be able to be helped by these things. There is a certain manner of living, neither so good that there is no need of these helps after death, nor yet so wicked that these helps are of no avail after death" (*Handbook on Faith, Hope, and Charity* 29:109).

III. THE SACRAMENTS

10. The Sacrament of Baptism and Its Effects

This Tradition stems from the teachings of Christ and the Apostles about the nature and effects of the sacrament of baptism. This is one of those spectacular examples of a Catholic Tradition that can be easily traced in its present form from today all the way back to the time of Christ and the Apostles, with essentially no change in the way the teaching was expressed then versus now. The witness of the early Church is clear that this doctrinal Tradition was explained and taught in the same terms as it is today. Before we look at the examples from the early Church that show this, let's set the stage by seeing what the Church teaches today on this subject.

The *Catechism* explains the fundamental issue at work in the Church's Tradition about the effects of the sacrament of baptism:

1. We are sacramentally "assimilated" into Christ through baptism; we are "reborn" of water and the Holy Spirit (cf. CCC 537, 628; Romans 6:4).
2. We are buried with Christ and raised to new life through his Resurrection; we die to sin and live, renewed, in the Spirit (cf. CCC 628; Romans 6:4; Colossians 2:12; Ephesians 5:26).
3. In baptism, the Holy Spirit cleanses us of all sin, original and actual, and He bestows sanctifying grace on us, the very life of the Trinity (cf. CCC 694; 1 Corinthians 12:13; John 4:10-14; 7:38; Exodus 17:1-6; Isaiah 55:1; Zechariah 14:8; 1 Corinthians 10:4; Revelation 21:6; 22:17).

The *Catechism* points us to the fact that the sacrament of baptism is no mere ordinance that simply symbolizes the washing of the soul. It actually does what it symbolizes. As St. Peter declared:

"For Christ also suffered for sins once, the righteous for the sake of the unrighteous, that he might lead you to God. Put to death in the flesh, he was brought to life in the spirit. In it he also went to preach to the spirits in prison, who had once been disobedient while God patiently waited in the days of Noah during the building of the ark, in which a few persons, eight in all, were saved through water. This prefigured baptism, which saves you now. It is not a removal of dirt from the body but an appeal to God for a clear conscience, through the resurrection of Jesus Christ . . ." (1 Peter 3:18-21).

The early Church echoed this teaching of St. Peter far and wide that "baptism saves you now." Some examples of this ancient Tradition of baptismal regeneration drawn from the Church Fathers are:

St. Gregory of Nazianzus — "Let us be buried with Christ by Baptism to rise with him; let us go down with him to be raised with him; and let us rise with him to be glorified with him" (*Oratio* 40).

St. Hilary of Poitiers — "Everything that happened to Christ lets us know that, after the bath of water, the Holy Spirit swoops down upon us from high heaven and that, adopted by the Father's voice, we become sons of God" (*On Matthew* 2, 5).

11. Infant Baptism

If you're Catholic, chances are you were baptized when you were only a few weeks old. This tradition of infant baptism is as old as the Catholic Church herself, and it's found in the earliest years of the Church's ministry. In fact, the Catholic tradition of infant baptism — something hotly objected to by many non-Catholic groups, especially by many Protestants — was a universal practice in the early Church. The reason this Tradition was so widespread from the very earliest days of the Church was because those first Christians who heard the Apostles directly, or who read their letters in the first and second generation, knew what the Apostles intended when it came to baptism. They knew that this sacrament, whether administered by immersion (dunking) or infusion (pouring), was both the normative way for entering the Church as well as the powerful means by which all original sin and actual sin was eradicated from the soul and the indwelling of the life of the Blessed Trinity itself (sanctifying grace) is infused into the soul.

In the Old Testament, circumcision was the imperfect forerunner of baptism. Through the Old Testament ordinance of circumcision, males formally entered into the Covenant with God. This requirement was incumbent on adults who converted as well as infant boys who were born into Jewish families (cf. Leviticus 12:2-3).

Obviously, the eight-day old infant could not ask for circumcision. His parents, rather, brought him to the Temple or synagogue to be circumcised and thereby covenanted with God *on behalf of their child*. God intended for it to be this way, and virtually all Jewish men were circumcised as infants, not as adults. This is an important parallel and link with the New Testament sacrament of baptism. The Lord elevated that ordinance to a new and perfected level of grace.

The early Christians new this well. They knew that the sacrament of baptism replaced the ordinance of circumcision (cf. Colossians 2:11-12). They knew the effects of baptism to regenerate, to wash away sin, and infuse sanctifying grace (cf. Acts 2:38, 22:16; Titus 3:5). They knew that the Old Covenant ordinance of circumcision, although it mirrored baptism imperfectly and only in anticipation, had no saving power (cf. Galatians 5:6, 6:15). But they new that the New Covenant "baptism now saves you" (1 Peter 3:21). "[W]hy do you wait?" St. Paul exhorted the early Christians. "Rise and be baptized, and wash away your sins, calling on his name" (Acts 22:16, RSV).

And they knew these things because they had received the Tradition of infant baptism from the Apostles themselves. No one could later on convince them that this or that passage in Scripture meant that only adults could be baptized (as Baptists and other Protestants imagine) because *they knew the meaning of those passages of Scripture as the Apostles intended them to be understood*. That is precisely the meaning of Tradition: the Christian Church living out her authentic understanding of the meaning of the inspired written and oral teaching of Christ and the Apostles.

Even a noted Protestant scholar and expert on the early Church recognized this fact as he wrote about the early Church's understanding of the saving power of baptism:

> "From the beginning baptism was the universally accepted rite of admission to the Church. Only 'those who have been baptized in the Lord's name'[54] [cf. Matthew 28:19-20] could partake of the Eucharist. As regards its significance, it was always held to convey the remission of sins . . ." (*Early Christian Doctrines* 193).

Let's consider some examples from the early Church that testify to the ancient Christian Tradition of infant baptism. In them we see many early Church bishops handing on the authentic understanding of the Traditions of baptismal regeneration and the baptism of infants. In their writings, these good men were fulfilling St. Paul's command to bishops:

"A bishop as God's steward . . . [must hold] fast to the true message as taught so that he will be able both to exhort with sound doctrine and to refute opponents" (Titus 1:7, 9).

The *Epistle of Barnabas*, A.D. 170 — "Regarding [baptism], we have the evidence of Scripture that Israel would refuse to accept the washing which confers the remission of sins and would set up a substitution of their own instead" (section 11).

Hermas, circa A.D. 140–155 — " 'I have heard, sir,' said I, 'from some teacher, that there is no other repentance except that which took place when we went down into the water and obtained the remission of our former sins.' He said to me, 'You have heard rightly, for so it is' " (*The Shepherd* 4:3:1).

St. Ignatius of Antioch, A.D. 107 — "Let none of you turn deserter. Let your baptism be your armor; your faith, your helmet; your love, your spear; your patient endurance, your panoply" (*Letter to Polycarp* 6).

St. Justin Martyr, A.D. 151 — "Whoever are convinced and believe that what they are taught and told by us is the truth, and profess to be able to live accordingly, are instructed to pray and to beseech God in fasting for the remission of their former sins, while we pray and fast with them. Then they are led by us to a place where there is water, and they are reborn in the same kind of rebirth in which we ourselves were reborn: 'In the name of God, the Lord and Father of all, and of our Savior Jesus Christ, and of the Holy

Spirit,' they receive the washing of water. For Christ said, 'Unless you be reborn, you shall not enter the kingdom of heaven' " (*First Apology* 61:14).

St. Justin Martyr — "As many as are persuaded and believe that what we [Christians] teach and say is true, and undertake to be able to live accordingly, and instructed to pray and to entreat God with fasting, for the remission of their sins that are past, we pray and fast with them. Then they are brought by us where there is water and are regenerated in the same manner in which we were ourselves regenerated. For, in the name of God, the Father . . . and of our Savior Jesus Christ, and of the Holy Spirit,[55] they then receive the washing with water. For Christ also said, 'Unless you are born again, you shall not enter into the kingdom of heaven' " (*First Apology* 61).

St. Irenaeus of Lyons, A.D. **190** — "'And [Naaman] dipped himself . . . seven times in the Jordan.'[56] It was not for nothing that Naaman of old, when suffering from leprosy, was purified upon his being baptized, but [this served] as an indication to us. For as we are lepers in sin, we are made clean, by means of the sacred water and the invocation of the Lord, from our old transgressions, being spiritually regenerated as new-born babes, even as the Lord has declared: 'Except a man be born again through water and the Spirit, he shall not enter into the kingdom of heaven' " (*Fragment* 34).

Theophilus of Antioch, A.D. **181** — "Moreover, those things which were created from the waters were blessed by God, so that this might also be a sign that men would at a future time receive repentance and remission of sins through water and the bath of regeneration all who proceed to the truth and are born again and receive a blessing from God" (*To Autolycus* 12:16).

St. Clement of Alexandria, A.D. **191** — "When we are baptized, we are enlightened. Being enlightened, we are adopted as sons. Adopted as sons, we are made perfect. Made perfect, we become immortal . . . 'and sons of the Most High' [Psalm 82:6]. This work is variously called grace, illumination, perfection, and washing. It is a washing by which we are cleansed of sins, a gift of grace by which the punishments due our sins are remitted, an illumination by which we behold that holy light of salvation" (*The Instructor of Children* 1:6:26:1).

Tertullian, A.D. 203 — "Happy is our sacrament of water, in that, by washing away the sins of our early blindness, we are set free and admitted into eternal life. . . . [But] a viper of the Cainite heresy, lately conversant in this quarter, has carried away a great number with her most venomous doctrine, making it her first aim to destroy baptism — which is quite in accordance with nature, for vipers and asps . . . themselves generally do live in arid and waterless places. But we, little fishes after the example of our Fish [i.e., which symbolizes], Jesus Christ, are born in water, nor have we safety in any other way than by permanently abiding in water. So that most monstrous creature, who had no right to teach even sound doctrine, knew full well how to kill the little fishes — by taking them away from the water!" (*On Baptism* 1).

St. Hippolytus, A.D. 215 — "And the bishop shall lay his hand upon them [the newly baptized], invoking and saying: 'O Lord God, who did count these worthy of deserving the forgiveness of sins by the laver of regeneration, make them worthy to be filled with your Holy Spirit and send upon them thy grace [in confirmation], that they may serve you according to your will' " (*The Apostolic Tradition* 22:1).

St. Cyprian of Carthage, circa A.D. 250 — "While I was lying in darkness . . . I thought it indeed difficult and hard to believe . . . that divine mercy was promised for my salvation, so that anyone might be born again and quickened unto a new life by the laver of the saving water, he might put off what he had been before, and, although the structure of the body remained, he might change himself in soul and mind. . . . But afterwards, when the stain of my past life had been washed away by means of the water of rebirth, a light from above poured itself upon my chastened and now pure heart; afterwards, through the Spirit which is breathed from heaven, a second birth made of me a new man" (*Epistle to Donatus* 3).

Origen, A.D. 248 — "The Church received from the apostles the tradition of giving baptism even to infants. For the apostles, to whom were committed the secrets of divine mysteries, knew that there is in everyone the innate stains of sin, which are washed away through water and the Spirit" (*Commentaries on Romans* 5:9).

St. Cyril of Jerusalem, A.D. 350 — "If any man does not receive baptism, he does not have salvation. The only exception is the martyrs, who, even without water, will receive baptism, for the Savior calls martyrdom a baptism.[57] . . . Bearing your sins, you go down into the water; but the calling down of grace seals your soul and does not permit that you afterwards be swallowed up by the fearsome dragon. You go down dead in your sins, and you come up made alive in righteousness" (*Catechetical Lectures* 3:10, 12).

St. Athanasius, A.D. 360 — "[A]s we are all from earth and die in Adam, so being regenerated from above of water and Spirit, in the Christ we are all quickened" (*Four Discourses Against the Arians* 3:26).

St. Basil the Great, A.D. 375 — "This then is what it means to be 'born again of water and Spirit': Just as our dying is effected in the water,[58] our living is wrought through the Spirit. In three immersions and an equal number of invocations the great mystery of baptism is completed in such a way that the type of death may be shown figuratively, and that by the handing on of divine knowledge the souls of the baptized may be illuminated. If, therefore, there is any grace in the water, it is not from the nature of water, but from the Spirit's presence there" (*The Holy Spirit* 15:35).

St. Basil the Great, A.D. 379 — "For prisoners, baptism is ransom, forgiveness of debts, the death of sin, regeneration of the soul, a resplendent garment, an unbreakable seal, a chariot to heaven, a royal protector, a gift of adoption" (*Sermons on Moral and Practical Subjects* 13).

The First Council of Constantinople, A.D. 381 — "We believe . . . in one baptism for the remission of sins" (*Nicene Creed*).

St. Ambrose of Milan, A.D. 389 — "The Lord was baptized, not to be cleansed himself but to cleanse the waters, so that those waters, cleansed by the flesh of Christ which knew no sin, might have the power of baptism. Whoever comes, therefore, to the washing of Christ lays aside his sins" (*Commentary on Luke* 2:83).

St. Augustine of Hippo, A.D. 412 — "It is an excellent thing that the Punic [North African] Christians call baptism salvation and the sacrament of Christ's Body nothing else than life. Whence does this derive, except from an ancient and, as I suppose, apostolic tradition, by which the Churches of Christ hold inherently that without baptism and participation at the table of the Lord it is impossible for any man to attain either to the kingdom of God or to salvation and life eternal? This is the witness of Scripture too. . . . The sacrament of baptism is most assuredly the sacrament of regeneration" (*Forgiveness and the Just Deserts of Sin* 1:24:34, and *The Baptism of Infants* 2:27:43).

St. Augustine of Hippo, A.D. 420 — "Baptism washes away all, absolutely all, our sins, whether of deed, word, or thought, whether sins original or added, whether knowingly or unknowingly contracted" (*Against Two Letters of the Pelagians* 3:3:5).

St. Augustine of Hippo, A.D. 421 — "This is the meaning of the great sacrament of baptism, which is celebrated among us: All who attain to this grace die thereby to sin — as he himself [Christ] is said to have died to sin because he died in the flesh (that is, 'in the likeness of sin') — and they are thereby alive by being reborn in the baptismal font, just as he rose again from the sepulcher. This is the case no matter what the age of the body. For whether it be a newborn infant or a decrepit old man — since no one should be barred from baptism — just so, there is no one who does not die to sin in baptism. Infants die to original sin only; adults, to all those sins which they have added, through their evil living, to the burden they brought with them at birth" (*Handbook on Faith, Hope, and Love* 13).

St. Jerome, A.D. 415 — "This much you must know, that baptism forgives past sins, but it does not safeguard future righteousness, which is preserved by labor and industry and diligence and depends always and above all on the mercy of God" (*Dialogue Against the Pelagians* 3:1).

12. The Three Modes of Baptism: Immersion, Infusion, and Sprinkling

The ancient Christian tradition of administering the sacrament of baptism — to infants and adults alike — took three distinct forms: immersion (dunking), infusion (pouring), and sprinkling. Perhaps the earliest extant testimonies to these different ways of baptizing are the *Epistle of Barnabas* and the *Didache*, a Middle-Eastern (probably Syrian) document that explains the teachings of the Church on various matters, including baptism and the other sacraments.

The *Epistle of Barnabas*, A.D. 70 — "Further, what does he say? 'And there was a river flowing on the right, and from it arose beautiful trees; and whosoever shall eat of them shall live for ever.' This means, that we indeed descend into the water [of baptism] full of sins and defilement, but come up, bearing fruit in our heart, having the fear [of God] and trust in Jesus in our spirit" (section 11).

The *Didache*, circa A.D. 140 — "Concerning baptism, baptize thus: Having first rehearsed all these things, 'baptize, in the Name of the Father and of the Son and of the Holy Spirit,' in running water; but if you have no running water, baptize in other water, and if you cannot [baptize] in cold, then in warm. But if you have neither, pour water three times on the head 'in the Name of the Father, Son and Holy Spirit.' And before the baptism let the baptizer and him who is to be baptized fast, and any others who are able. And thou shalt bid him who is to be baptized [i.e., an adult] to fast one or two days before" (section 7).

St. Hippolytus of Rome, A.D. 215 — "At dawn, a prayer shall be offered over the water. Where there is no scarcity of water the stream shall flow through the baptismal font or pour into it from above. But if water is scarce, whether as a constant condition or on occasion, then use whatever water is available" (*The Apostolic Tradition* 21).

Pope St. Cornelius of Rome, A.D. 251 — "As [Novatian] seemed about to die, he received baptism in the bed where he lay, by pouring" (*Letter to Fabius of Antioch*).

St. Cyprian of Carthage, A.D. 255 — "You have asked also, dearest son, what I thought of those who obtain God's grace in sickness and weakness, whether they are to be accounted legitimate Christians, for that they are not to be washed [i.e., immersed], but sprinkled, with the saving water. In this point, my diffidence and modesty prejudges none, so as to prevent any from feeling what he thinks right, and from doing what he feels to be right.

"As far as my poor understanding conceives it, I think that the divine benefits can in no respect be mutilated and weakened; nor can anything less occur in that case, where, with full and entire faith both of the giver and receiver, is accepted what is drawn from the divine gifts. For in the sacrament of salvation the contagion of sins is not in such wise washed away, as the filth of the skin and of the body is washed away in the carnal and ordinary washing. . . . In the sacraments of salvation, when necessity compels, and God bestows His mercy, the divine methods confer the whole benefit on believers; nor ought it to trouble any one that sick people seem to be sprinkled or affused [i.e., water poured over their heads], when they obtain the Lord's grace, when Holy Scripture speaks by the mouth of the prophet Ezekiel, and says, 'Then will I *sprinkle* clean water upon you, and ye shall be clean: from all your filthiness and from all your idols will I cleanse you. And I will give you a new heart, and a new spirit will I put within you.' . . . And again: 'And the Lord spake unto Moses saying, Take the Levites from among the children of Israel, and cleanse them. And thus shalt thou do unto them, to cleanse them: *thou shalt sprinkle them with the water of purification.*

"And again: 'The water of sprinkling is a purification.' Whence it appears that the sprinkling also of water prevails equally with the washing of salvation;

and that when this is done in the Church, where the faith both of receiver and giver is sound, all things hold and may be consummated and perfected by the majesty of the Lord and by the truth of faith" (*Letter to Magnus* 12; emphasis mine).[59]

13. Confession to a Priest

This Tradition is the age-old doctrine that in the sacrament of penance (i.e., confession, reconciliation), the priest has the authority, given him by Christ in virtue of his ordination, to forgive sins committed after baptism of those who confess to him. The priestly action of sacramentally forgiving the sins of a penitent is always and only a function of Christ's priestly power, which is exercised through the ministry of the priest.

The doctrinal Tradition of confessing one's sins to a priest is one that frequently comes under attack from non-Catholics, especially Protestants. The fact is, though, the teaching that the faithful should confess their sins to the priests stems not from human sources, but from God himself. It was Jesus Christ who declared to his Apostles: "He whose sins you forgive are forgiven him, and he whose sins you retain, are retained [i.e., not absolved]" (John 20:22-23). There are other biblical passages we can examine to demonstrate this truth,[60] but for the moment, let's concentrate on the fact that here we see Christ confer the authority to forgive sins, *but he does not provide the ability to read the minds of those who wish their sins to be forgiven*. In other words, for the apostle (and by extension, his successors in the priestly ministry he received from the Lord, namely the bishops and priests of all generations) to be able to exercise the authority given him by Christ the penitent had to confess those sins.

If he didn't, the power conferred by Christ to forgive sins would have been moot and superfluous, hardly the kind of thing we know Christ to do. Keep this fact clearly in mind when the issue of confession to a priest comes up: Jesus Christ arranged things so that the sacramental forgiveness of sins would come through the ministry of the priest. If someone argues against that Tradition, he's really arguing not so much against the Catholic Church, but against Christ himself. And that is a very dangerous position to put oneself in. The Lord promised his Apostles, "Whoever listens to you listens to me. Whoever rejects you rejects me" (Luke 10:16, NAB).

The Council of Trent explained the essential elements of the Tradition of confession of sins to a priest:

"As a means of regaining grace and justice, penance was at all times necessary for those who had defiled their souls with any mortal sin. . . . Before the coming of Christ, penance was not a sacrament, nor is it since His coming a sacrament for those who are not baptized. But the Lord then principally instituted the Sacrament of Penance, when, being raised from the dead, he breathed upon His disciples saying: 'Receive ye the Holy Ghost. Whose sins you shall forgive, they are forgiven them; and whose sins you shall retain, they are retained' (John 20:22-23). By which action so signal and words so clear the consent of all the Fathers has ever understood that the power of forgiving and retaining sins was communicated to the Apostles and to their lawful successors, for the reconciling of the faithful who have fallen after Baptism" (session 14).

Confession to a priest involves several elements: First, a verbal disclosure of one's sins. Second, the action of sacramental forgiveness by the priest (i.e., absolution) by whom God grants "pardon and peace" to the sinner. Third, God reconciles the sinner to himself and to the Church (cf. 2 Corinthians 5:20; Matthew 5:24; cf. CCC 1424).

The Christian Tradition of auricular confession is well attested to in the writings of the early Church. In addition to the express declaration of Christ in John 20:20-23, in which he says, "He whose sins you forgive are forgiven him, and he whose sins you retain are retained,"[61] we also hear the echo of this teaching, years later, in the writings of St. Paul:

> "All this is from God, who through Christ reconciled us to himself and gave us the ministry of reconciliation; that is, in Christ God was reconciling the world to himself, not counting their trespasses against them, and entrusting to us the message of reconciliation. So we are ambassadors for Christ, God making his appeal through us. We beseech you on behalf of Christ, be reconciled to God" (2 Corinthians 5:18-20, RSV).

The theological terminology of the early Church centered on three often used words for this sacrament: the Latin *penitentia* and the corresponding Greek terms *metanoia* and *exomologesis.* This language of the need for personal conversion, repentance, and then confession of one's sins to the priests is present very early. The *Didache*, for example, is an anonymous but authoritative early Christian document written at the close of the first century. Consider its statements about the sacrament of confession. It provides a clear snapshot of the teaching of the Church at that time regarding confession to a priest:

> "In the congregation thou shalt confess thy transgressions, and thou shalt not betake thyself to prayer

with an evil conscience. This is the Way of Life" (*Didache* 4:14).

"On the Lord's Day[62] of the Lord come together, break bread and hold the Eucharist, after confessing your transgressions that your offering may be pure; but let none who has a quarrel with his fellow join in your meeting until they are reconciled, that your sacrifice [i.e., the Eucharistic sacrifice of the Mass] be not defiled" (*Didache* 14:1).

The Church Fathers speak often about this sacrament of confession:

Pope St. Clement of Rome, circa A.D. 80-96 — "Ye therefore, who laid the foundation of this sedition, submit yourselves to the presbyters, and receive correction so as to repent, bending the knees of your hearts. Learn to be subject [i.e., to the presbyters], laying aside the proud and arrogant self-confidence of your tongue" (*Epistle to the Corinthians* 57).

St. Cyprian of Carthage, died A.D. 258 — "Let each confess his sin while he is still in this world, while his confession can be received, while satisfaction and the forgiveness granted by the priests is acceptable to God" (*On the Lapsed* 29).

St. Ambrose of Milan, A.D. 340-397 — "They [i.e., the Montanist heretics] affirm that they are showing great reverence for God, to Whom alone they reserve the power of forgiving sins. But in truth none do Him greater injury than they who choose to prune His commandments and reject the office entrusted to them [i.e., to the priests]. For inasmuch as the Lord Jesus Himself said in the Gospel: 'Receive ye the Holy Spirit, whosesoever sins ye forgive they are forgiven unto them, and whosesoever sins ye retain, they are retained,' Who is it that honors Him most, he who obeys His bidding or he who rejects it?

"The Church holds fast its obedience on either side, by both retaining and remitting sin; heresy is on the one side cruel, and on the other disobedient; wishes to bind what it will not loosen, and will not loosen what it has bound, whereby it condemns itself by its own sentence. For the Lord willed that the power of binding and of loosing should be alike, and sanctioned each by a similar condition. So he who has not the power to loose has not the power to bind. For as, according to the Lord's word, he who has the power to bind has also the power to loose, their teaching destroys itself, inasmuch as they who deny that they have the power of loosing ought also to deny that of binding. For how can the one be allowed and the other disallowed? It is plain and evident that either each is allowed or each is disallowed in the case of those to whom each has been given. Each is allowed to the Church, neither to heresy, for this power has been entrusted to priests alone. Rightly, therefore, does the Church claim it, which has true priests; heresy, which has not the priests of God, cannot claim it. And by not claiming this power heresy pronounces its own sentence, that not possessing priests it cannot claim priestly power. And so in their shameless obstinacy a shamefaced acknowledgment meets our view.

"Consider, too, the point that he who has received the Holy Ghost [i.e., through the imposition of hands in ordination] has also received the power of forgiving and of retaining sin. For thus it is written: 'Receive the Holy Spirit: whosoever sins ye forgive, they are forgiven unto them, and whosoever sins ye retain, they are retained.' So, then, he who has not received power to forgive sins has not received the Holy Spirit. The office of the priest is a gift of the Holy Spirit, and His right it is specially to forgive and to retain sins. How, then, can they [i.e., the Novatianists] claim His gift who distrust His power and His right?" (*Two Books Concerning Penance* 1:5-8).

St. Augustine of Hippo — "Let us not listen to those who deny that the Church of God has the power to forgive all sins" (*On the Agony of Christ*, 3).

St. Pacian of Barcelona, died A.D. 390 — "This [i.e., granting absolution], you say, only God can do. Quite true: but what He does through His priests is the doing of His own power" (*First Epistle to Sympronianus* 6).

St. Cyril of Alexandria, died A.D. 447 — "Men filled with the spirit of God forgive sins in two ways, either by admitting to baptism those who are worthy or by pardoning the penitent children of the Church" (*On John* 1:12).

St. John Chrysostom, A.D. 347–407 — "Not only when they [the priests] regenerate us [through baptism], but also after our new birth, they can forgive us our sins" (*De sacred*. 3:5).

St. Athanasius, died A.D. 373 — "As the man whom the priest baptizes is enlightened by the grace of the Holy Ghost, so does he who in penance confesses his sins, receive through the priest forgiveness in virtue of the grace of Christ" (*Against Novatian*).

Pope St. Leo the Great, reigned A.D. 440–461 — "The manifold mercy of God so assists men when they fall, that not only by the grace of baptism but also by the remedy of penitence is the hope of eternal life revived, in order that they who have violated the gifts of the second birth, condemning themselves by their own judgment, may attain to remission of their crimes, the provisions of the Divine Goodness having so ordained that God's indulgence cannot be obtained without the supplications of priests. For the Mediator between God and men, the Man Christ Jesus, has transmitted this power to those that are set over the Church that they should both grant a course of penitence to those who confess, and, when they are cleansed by wholesome correction admit them through the door of reconciliation to communion in the sacraments. . . .

"Hazardous as deathbed repentance is, the grace of absolution must not be refused even when it can be asked for only by signs. Hence it behooves each individual Christian to listen to the judgment of his own conscience, lest he put off the turning to God from day to day and fix the time of his amendment at the end of his life; for it is most perilous for human frailty and ignorance to confine itself to such conditions as to be reduced to the uncertainty of a few hours, and instead of winning indulgence by fuller amendment, to choose the narrow limits of that time when space is scarcely found even for the penitent's confession or the priest's absolution. But, as I have said, even such men's needs must be so assisted that the free action of penitence and the grace of communion be not denied them, if they demand it even when their voice is gone, by the signs of a still clear intellect. And if they be so overcome by the stress of their malady that they cannot signify in the priest's presence what just before they were asking for, the testimony of believers standing by must prevail for them, that they may obtain the benefit of penitence and reconciliation simultaneously. . ." (*Epistle 108, To Theodore, Bishop of Forum Julii*).

We can see from those few examples of the many that could be adduced that the early Church was keenly aware of the priest's sacramental authority to forgive sins in the name of Jesus Christ. And this realization was an echo in the post-apostolic era of the Tradition of the sacrament of confession that was taught by Christ and the Apostles.

14. The Eucharistic Liturgy

The Catholic term "Liturgy" derives from the Greek word *leitourgia*, which means "a public duty" or "a public action." This meaning took on a religious connotation in regard to the public ministrations of the Old Testament priests in the Temple (cf. Exodus 38:27, 39:12; Joel 1:9, 2:17; where the term *leitourgeo* is used in the Greek, Septuagint, version). The ancient Tradition of the Liturgy has been taught and believed by Christians since the days of Christ. Latin Rite Catholics are accustomed to referring to it as the "Mass," while Eastern Catholics call it the "Divine Liturgy." Both refer to the same doctrine.

Since the night Christ was betrayed, the Catholic Church has been celebrating the Liturgy of the Eucharist. This is part of Sacred Tradition, a revealed doctrine of the Faith that came from Christ himself and was preached and taught by the Apostles and their successors from the earliest days of the Church. About the year 56, St. Paul wrote about this Tradition and of how important it was to the life of the Church:

> "I praise you because you remember me in everything and hold fast to the traditions,[63] just as I handed them on to you. . . ."

For the first few centuries, the Eucharistic Liturgy was not a formally codified ritual as we know it today, though it was universally celebrated in the East and West with its essential elements and according to the particular meaning the Catholic Church has always understood it to contain: the once-for-all sacrifice of Christ on the cross, re-presented in time and space.

The *Catechism* explains the Church's meaning when it refers to the Church's Tradition of the Eucharistic Liturgy, defining it to mean:

> *An action of thanksgiving to God* (CCC 1328);
> *The Lord's Supper* (CCC 1329; cf. 1 Corinthians 11:20; Revelation 19:9);
> *The Breaking of Bread* (CCC 1329; cf. Matthew 14:19, 15:36, 26:26; Mark 8:6, 19.);
> *The Eucharistic assembly* (CCC 1329; cf. 1 Corinthians 11:17-34);
> *The memorial of the Lord's Passion and Resurrection* (CCC 1330);
> *A Holy Sacrifice* (CCC 1330; cf. Hebrews 13:15; cf. 1 Peter 2:5; Psalm 116:13, 17; Malachi 1:11);
> *The Holy and Divine Liturgy*;
> *Holy Communion* (CCC 1331; cf. 1 Corinthians 10:16-17);
> *Holy Mass* (CCC 1332).

From these explanatory sections from the *Catechism*, we can see the essential elements of the Tradition of the Eucharistic Liturgy. This has been an ever-present, ubiquitous Tradition in the Church since the time of Christ and the Apostles. What makes this Tradition so powerful when a Catholic dialogues with Protestants is that it is undeniable that the early Christians did not gather for a "Sunday service," as Protestants typically understand the term. Rather, the early Christians gathered together to celebrate the Eucharistic sacrifice, complete with the essential prayers and gestures we use today in the Catholic Church (as well as in the Eastern Catholic and Orthodox Churches).

15. The Mass as a Sacrifice

Since the time of the Apostles, the Catholic Church has taught that the Eucharistic Liturgy (i.e., the Mass) is a holy sacrifice — the "once for all" sacrifice of Christ on the cross represented in time and space in an unbloody manner. It is not a new or different sacrifice from the one that Christ accomplished on Calvary. It is the mystical participation in which all members of the Body of Christ are called to participate, just as our brothers and sisters in heaven are, even now, participating in it. Christ's perfect sacrifice on the cross is perpetuated across time in and through the Mass, which is our earthly participation in the heavenly liturgy where Christ, the eternal high priest, perpetually offers himself as a perfect sacrifice to the Father on our behalf (cf. CCC 1370).

If you get onto the subject of the Mass with an Evangelical or Fundamentalist Protestant, you're likely to be hit with the argument that Christ died "once for all" (cf. Hebrews 10:10). "And if, as the Bible so clearly says, he died 'once for all,' " the Protestant will argue, "how can the Catholic Church possibly justify its tradition that the Mass is the 'unbloody sacrifice of Christ on Calvary'?"

This is a good question, and it deserves a good answer. First, keep in mind that the Church does not now nor has it ever taught that the Mass is "another" sacrifice or a "different" sacrifice or some kind of a "repeat" of the "once for all" sacrifice of Christ on the Cross. No. The Holy Sacrifice of the Mass is the one, same, unique, eternal, "once for all" sacrifice of Christ represented for us in space and time.

Now let's consider these representative examples of what this Tradition was in the Church and why

Christians since the time of the Apostles have believed in this Tradition.

The *Didache*, circa A.D. 70 — "Assemble on the Lord's day, and break bread and offer the Eucharist, but first make confession of your faults, so that your sacrifice may be a pure one. Anyone who has a difference with his fellow is not to take part with you until they have been reconciled, so as to avoid any profanation of your sacrifice.[64] For this is the offering of which the Lord has said, 'Everywhere and always bring me a sacrifice that is undefiled, for I am a great king, says the Lord, and my name is the wonder of nations' "[65] (section 14).

Pope St. Clement of Rome, circa A.D. 80 — "Our sin will not be small if we eject from the episcopate those who blamelessly and holily have offered its sacrifices. Blessed are those presbyters who have already finished their course, and who have obtained a fruitful and perfect release" (*Epistle to the Corinthians*, 44:4-5).

St. Ignatius of Antioch, A.D. 107 — "Make certain, therefore, that you all observe one common Eucharist; for there is but one Body of our Lord Jesus Christ, and but one cup of union with his Blood, and one single altar of sacrifice — even as there is also but one bishop, with his clergy and my own fellow servitors, the deacons. This will ensure that all your doings are in full accord with the will of God" (*Epistle to the Philadelphians* 4).

St. Justin Martyr, A.D. 155 — "God speaks by the mouth of Malachi, one of the twelve [minor prophets], as I said before, about the sacrifices at that time presented by you: 'I have no pleasure in you, says the Lord, and I will not accept your sacrifices at your hands; for from the rising of the sun to the going down of the same, my name has been glorified among the

Gentiles, and in every place incense is offered to my name, and a pure offering, for my name is great among the Gentiles' [cf. Malachi 1:10-11]. He then speaks of those Gentiles, namely us, who in every place offer sacrifices to him, that is, the bread of the Eucharist and also the cup of the Eucharist" (*Dialogue Against Trypho the Jew* 41).

St. Irenaeus of Lyons, A.D. **189** — "He took from among creation that which is bread, and gave thanks, saying, 'This is my body.' The cup likewise, which is from among the creation to which we belong, he confessed to be his blood. He taught the new sacrifice of the new covenant, of which Malachi, one of the twelve [minor] prophets, had signified beforehand: 'You do not do my will, says the Lord Almighty, and I will not accept a sacrifice at your hands. For from the rising of the sun to its setting my name is glorified among the Gentiles, and in every place incense is offered to my name, and a pure sacrifice; for great is my name among the gentiles, says the Lord Almighty' [cf. Malachi 1:10-11]. By these words he makes it plain that the former people will cease to make offerings to God; but that in every place sacrifice will be offered to him, and indeed, a pure one, for his name is glorified among the Gentiles" (*Against Heresies*, 4:17:5).

St. Cyprian of Carthage, A.D. **253** — "If Christ Jesus, our Lord and God, is himself the high priest of God the Father; and if he offered himself as a sacrifice to the Father; and if he commanded that this be done in commemoration of himself, then certainly the priest, who imitates that which Christ did, truly functions in place of Christ" (Letter 62, *To Caecilius on the Sacrament of the Cup of the Lord* 14).

St. Cyril of Jerusalem, A.D. **350** — "Then, having sanctified ourselves by these spiritual hymns, we beseech the merciful God to send forth his Holy Spirit upon the gifts lying before him, that he may make the bread the Body of Christ and the wine the Blood of Christ, for whatsoever the Holy Spirit has touched is surely sanctified and changed. Then, upon the completion of the spiritual sacrifice, the bloodless worship, over that propitiatory victim we call upon God for the common peace of the churches, for the welfare of the world, for kings, for soldiers and allies, for the sick, for the afflicted; and in summary, we all pray and offer this sacrifice for all who are in need" (*Catechetical Lectures* 23:7-8).

St. John Chrysostom, A.D. 387 — "When you see the Lord immolated and lying upon the altar, and the priest bent over that sacrifice praying, and all the people empurpled by that precious blood, can you think that you are still among men and on earth? Or are you not lifted up to heaven?" (*On the Priesthood* 3:4:177).

St. John Chrysostom, A.D. 391 — "Reverence this table, of which we are all communicants! Christ, slain for us, the sacrificial victim who is placed thereon!" (*Homilies on Romans* 8:8).

St. John Chrysostom, A.D. 403 — "Do we not offer [the Mass] daily? Yes, we offer, but making remembrance of his death; and this remembrance is one and not many. How is it one and not many? Because this sacrifice is offered once, like that in the Holy of Holies. This sacrifice is a type of that, and this remembrance a type of that. We offer always the same, not one sheep now and another tomorrow, but the same thing always. Thus there is one sacrifice. By this reasoning, since the sacrifice is offered everywhere, are there, then, a multiplicity of Christs? By no means! Christ is one everywhere. He is complete here, complete there, one body. And just as he is one body and not many though offered everywhere, so too is there one sacrifice" (*Homilies on Hebrews* 17:3).

St. Ambrose of Milan, A.D. **389** — "We saw the prince of priests coming to us, we saw and heard him offering his blood for us. We follow, inasmuch as we are able, being priests, and we offer the sacrifice on behalf of the people. Even if we are of but little merit, still, in the sacrifice, we are honorable. Even if Christ is not now seen as the one who offers the sacrifice, nevertheless it is he himself that is offered in sacrifice here on Earth when the body of Christ is offered. Indeed, to offer himself he is made visible in us, he whose word makes holy the sacrifice that is offered" (*Commentaries on Twelve Psalms of David* 38:25).

St. Augustine of Hippo, A.D. **419** — Ecclesiastes 2:24 says, "'There is no good for a man except that he should eat and drink,' what can he be more credibly understood to say than what belongs to the participation of this table which the Mediator of the New Testament himself, the priest after the order of Melchizedek, furnishes with his own body and blood? For that sacrifice has succeeded all the sacrifices of the Old Testament, which were slain as a shadow of what was to come. . . . Because, instead of all these sacrifices and oblations, his body is offered and is served up to the partakers of it" (*The City of God* 17:20).

16. Transubstantiation and the Real Presence

The Catholic Church teaches that at the moment of Consecration in the Mass, the substance of the bread and wine are, by the power of Christ working in and through the priest, changed into the Body and Blood as well as the soul and divinity of Christ. This is called the "Real Presence," and though the accidents (i.e., the outward physical characteristics that can be perceived by the senses) remain intact, the substance (i.e., the inward reality of a thing that cannot be perceived by the senses) has been transformed into the Body and Blood of the Lord. The reality of the Eucharistic bread and wine have vanished.

This is among the most ancient of Traditions in the Catholic Church; so ancient, in fact, that we can trace it clearly all the way to the mid-point of Jesus Christ's public ministry. So before we consider the way in which this Tradition took form and developed in the early Church, let's first pause for a moment and look at what Christ himself said about this Tradition.

In his "Bread of Life" discourse, the Lord emphasized several key elements of his teaching about the Eucharist:

First, Christ identifies himself as the Eucharist[66] when he said repeatedly, "I am the bread of life. Your fathers ate the manna in the wilderness, and they died. This is the bread which comes down from heaven, that a man may eat of it and not die. I am the living bread which came down from heaven; if any one eats of this bread, he will live for ever; and the bread which I shall give for the life of the world is my flesh" (John 6:48–51).

Second, Jesus ruled out a metaphorical or symbolic interpretation when he emphasized to those who were grumbling about his teaching, "My flesh is true food, and my blood is true drink. Whoever eats my flesh and drinks my blood remains in me and I in him. Just as the living Father sent me and I have life because of the Father, so also the one who feeds on me will have life because of me" (John 6:55–57). He said this in response to those who were agitated by his teaching and saying to each other, "How can this man give us his flesh to eat?" (John 6:52, RSV).

And third, the Lord spends a very long time explaining this truth to his followers. He is not bothered by the fact that many decide to leave him over this issue. Similarly, today, Catholics are often ridiculed or argued against by non-Catholics who deny the Real Presence in the Eucharist. We should always follow the Lord's example of standing firm in our proclamation of this truth, even if it means opposition or rejection.

St. Paul reinforces the fact that this Tradition of Christ's Real Presence in the Eucharist was understood by the earliest Christians to be literal, not metaphorical or symbolic: "I praise you because you remember me in everything and hold fast to the traditions, just as I handed them on to you. . . . For I received from the Lord what I also handed on to you, that the Lord Jesus, on the night he was handed over, took bread, and, after he had given thanks, broke it and said, 'This is my body that is for you. Do this in remembrance of me.' In the same way also the cup, after supper, saying, 'This cup is the new covenant in my blood. Do this, as often as you drink it, in remembrance of me' " (1 Corinthians 11:2, 23-25).

Commenting on this passage and the related passages in the Gospels that tell about the Last Supper, the early Christian writer Bishop Theodore of Mopsuestia wrote around the year 405 about the Tradition of the Real Presence of Christ in the Eucharist:

"When [Jesus Christ] gave the bread he did not say, 'This is the symbol of my body,' but, 'This is my body.' In the same way, when he gave the cup of his blood he did not say, 'This is the symbol of my blood,' but, 'This is my blood,' for he wanted us to look upon [the bread and the wine confected in the Eucharistic Liturgy], after their reception of grace and the coming of the Holy Spirit, not according to their nature, but to receive them as they are, the body and blood of our Lord" (*Catechetical Homilies* 5:1).

And that statement of this early Christian writer shows that though the technical theological term "transubstantiation" was not yet present in the vocabulary of the Church[67] the meaning behind the term definitely was.

Similar witnesses to the ancient Christian belief in the Real Presence can be cited in abundance. Here are several representative examples:

St. Ignatius of Antioch, circa A.D. 107 — "I have no taste for corruptible food nor for the pleasures of this life. I desire the bread of God, which is the flesh of Jesus Christ, who was of the seed of David; and for drink I desire his blood, which is love incorruptible" (*Epistle to the Romans* 7:3).

St. Ignatius of Antioch — "Take note of those who hold heterodox opinions on the grace of Jesus Christ which has come to us, and see how contrary their opinions are to the mind of God. . . . They abstain from the Eucharist and from prayer because they do not confess that the Eucharist is the flesh of our Savior Jesus Christ, flesh which suffered for our sins and which that Father, in his goodness, raised up again. They who deny the gift of God are perishing in their disputes" (*Epistle to the Smyrneans* 6:2—7:1).

St. Justin Martyr, A.D. 151 — "We call this food Eucharist, and no one else is permitted to partake of it, except one who believes our teaching to be true and who has been washed in the washing which is for the remission of sins and for regeneration and is thereby living as Christ enjoined. For not as common bread nor common drink do we receive these; but since Jesus Christ our Savior was made incarnate by the word of God and had both flesh and blood for our salvation, so too, as we have been taught, the food which has been made into the Eucharist by the Eucharistic prayer set down by him, and by the change of which our blood and flesh is nurtured, is both the flesh and the blood of that incarnated Jesus" (*First Apology* 66).

St. Irenaeus of Lyons, A.D. 180 — "If the Lord were from other than the Father, how could he rightly take bread, which is of the same creation as our own, and confess it to be his body and affirm that the mixture in the cup is his blood? . . . He has declared the cup, a part of creation, to be his own blood, from which he causes our blood to flow; and the bread, a part of creation, he has established as his own body, from which he gives increase unto our bodies. When, therefore, the mixed cup [wine and water] and the baked bread receives the Word of God and becomes the Eucharist, the body of Christ, and from these the substance of our flesh is increased and supported, how can they say that the flesh is not capable of receiving the gift of God, which is eternal life — flesh which is nourished by the body and blood of the Lord, and is in fact a member of him?" (*Against Heresies* 4:33-32, 5:2).

St. Cyril of Jerusalem, A.D. 350 — "The bread and the wine of the Eucharist before the holy invocation of the adorable Trinity were simple bread and wine, but the invocation having been made, the bread becomes the body of Christ and the wine the blood of Christ. . . . Do not, therefore, regard the bread and wine as simply that; for they are, according to the Master's declaration, the body and blood of Christ. Even though the senses suggest to you the other, let faith make you firm. Do not judge in this matter by taste, but be fully assured by the faith, not doubting that you have been deemed worthy of the body and blood of Christ . . . [being] fully convinced that the apparent bread is not bread, even though it is sensible to the taste, but the body of Christ, and that the apparent wine is not wine, even though the taste would have it so, . . . partake of that bread as something spiritual, and put a cheerful face on your soul" (*Catechetical Lectures* 19:7, 22:6, 9).

St. Ambrose of Milan, A.D. 390 — "Perhaps you may be saying, 'I see something else [when you look at the Eucharistic elements]; how is it that you assert that I receive the Body of Christ?' And this is the point which remains for us to prove. And what evidence shall we make use of? Let us prove that this is not what nature made, but what the blessing consecrated, and the power of blessing is greater than that of nature, because by blessing nature itself is changed. . . . We observe, then, that grace has more power than nature, and yet so far we have only spoken of the grace of a prophet's [i.e., Moses] blessing. But if the blessing of man had such power as to change nature, what are we to say of that divine consecration where the very words of the Lord and Savior operate? For that sacrament which you receive is made what it is by the word of Christ. . . . [T]he Church, beholding so great grace, exhorts her sons and her friends to come together to the sacraments, saying, 'Eat, my friends, and drink and be inebriated, my brother.' What we eat and what we drink the Holy Spirit has elsewhere made plain by the prophet, saying, 'Taste and see that the Lord is good, blessed is the man who hopes in Him.' Christ is in that sacrament; because it is the Body of Christ, it is therefore not bodily food but spiritual" (*The Mysteries* 9:50, 58).

St. Augustine of Hippo, circa A.D. **410 —** "Christ was carried in his own hands when, referring to his own Body, he said, 'This is my Body.'[68] For he carried that body in his hands" (*Expositions on the Psalms* 33:1:10).

St. Augustine of Hippo, A.D. **411 —** "I promised you who have now been baptized a sermon in which I would explain the sacrament of the Lord's Table, which you now look upon and of which you last night were made participants. You ought to know that you have received, what you are going to receive, and what you ought to receive daily. That bread which you see on the altar, having been sanctified by the word of God, is the Body of Christ. That chalice, or rather, what is in that chalice, having been sanctified by the word of God, is the Blood of Christ. . . . What you see is the bread and the chalice; that is what your own eyes report to you. But what your faith obliges you to accept is that the bread is the Body of Christ and the chalice is the Blood of Christ. This has been said very briefly, which may perhaps be sufficient for faith; yet faith does not desire instruction" (*Sermon* 272).

These representative excerpts from the early Church Fathers are excellent "monuments of Tradition," showing forth from the earliest days of the Church the consistent and universal belief among the early Christians in the teaching of Transubstantiation and the Real Presence of Christ in the Eucharist.

IV. CUSTOMS AND PRACTICES

17. Statues and Icons

The Christian use of icons, statues, and other sacred images is a useful way to recall the heavenly realities we are unable to perceive with our physical senses. Used properly, and with an utter avoidance of the sin of idolatry, icons and sacred images are in the Tradition of the Church because they help order our minds and hearts toward heaven, they remind us of the heroes of our Faith who have run the race before us and are now in heaven as a "cloud of witnesses" (Hebrews 12:1), and they help to express the doctrine that Christ himself is the "icon of the Living God" (Colossians 1:15).

The English word "icon" comes from the Greek word *eikonos* which literally means a "portrait" or an "image." Strictly speaking, an icon is a depiction of Christ, or Mary, or one of the angels and saints that is painted on wood. We may use the term, though, in a looser sense, to also include other sacred images, such as paintings and frescoes that are in many churches around the world painted directly onto the interior walls of a church. And by extension, the theology of the icon as a component of Catholic Tradition underlies the meaning of carved images, such as statues, bas-relief engravings, crucifixes, and other similar objects.

The *Catechism of the Catholic Church* says that icons are:

"[S]igns in the liturgical celebrations [that] are related to Christ: as are sacred images of the holy Mother of God and of the saints as well. They truly signify Christ, who is glorified in them. They make manifest the 'cloud of witnesses' [*Heb* 12:1] who continue to participate in the salvation of the world and to whom we are united, above all in sacramental celebrations. Through their icons, it is man 'in the image of God' [cf. Genesis 1:25-27], finally transfigured 'into his likeness' [cf. Romans 8:29, 1 John 3:2], who is revealed to our faith. So too are the angels, who also are recapitulated in Christ:

"Following the divinely inspired teaching of our holy Fathers and the Tradition of the Catholic Church (for we know that this tradition comes from the Holy Spirit who dwells in her) we rightly define with full certainty and correctness that, like the figure of the precious and life-giving cross, venerable and holy images of our Lord and God and Savior, Jesus Christ, our inviolate Lady, the holy Mother of God, and the venerated angels, all the saints and the just, whether painted or made of mosaic or another suitable material, are to be exhibited in the holy churches of God, on sacred vessels and vestments, walls and panels, in houses and on streets [Council of Nicaea II: DS 600]" (CCC 1161).

St. John of Damascus (676—circa 754-787), the great patriarch defender of this ancient Christian Tradition against the errors of the Iconoclasts, once wrote, "The beauty of the images moves me to contemplation, as a meadow delights the eyes and subtly infuses the soul with the glory of God" (*On the Holy Images* 1:27). His writings in defense of icons drew heavily on Sacred Scripture, Tradition, and his encyclopedic knowledge of the writings of the early Church Fathers, in part on the earlier work of Epiphanius of Salamis (cf. *Panarion*). Among his many superb explanations in defense of the holy icons was his exegesis of Colossians 1:15, where St. Paul describes Jesus as the "*image* of the living God." The Greek word used here for "image" is *eikon*, from which we derive the English word "icon." As St. John of Damascus pointed out in his defense of Tradition, if God himself would deign to come to us in the "image" of Christ, the second Person of the Trinity, it is clear that it is permissible for Christians to have images such as crucifixes, icons, and other sacred images to remind us of Christ and the saints in heaven.

At the height of the eighth-century Iconoclastic crisis (Iconoclasm — from the Greek for "image breaking" — the heretical movement that attempted to overthrow the ancient Christian practice of venerating the images and icons of Christ and the saints), a general council was called in 787 to deal with the problem. Empress Irene called the council after she requested that the pope either attend or send his personal representatives so that the council would be both legitimate and deemed ecumenical.

In that year the Second Council of Nicaea made its famous dogmatic pronouncement regarding the usefulness and goodness of sacred images and icons in the life of the Church, especially in its sacramental life:

"All the signs in the liturgical celebrations are related to Christ: as are sacred images of the holy Mother of God and of the saints as well. They truly signify Christ, who is glorified in them. They make manifest the 'cloud of witnesses' [cf. Hebrews 12:1] who continue to participate in the salvation of the world and to whom we are united, above all in sacramental celebrations. Through their icons, it is man 'in the image of God,' finally transfigured 'into his likeness' [cf. Romans 8:29 and 1 John 3:2] who is revealed to our faith. So too are the angels, who also are recapitulated in Christ: Following the divinely inspired teaching of our holy Fathers and the tradition of the Catholic Church (for we know that this tradition comes from the Holy Spirit who dwells in her) we rightly define with full certainty and correctness that, like the figure of the precious and life-giving cross, venerable and holy images of our Lord and God and Savior, Jesus Christ, our inviolate Lady, the holy Mother of God, and the venerated angels, all the saints and the just, whether painted or made of mosaic or another suitable material, are to be exhibited in the holy churches of God, on sacred vessels and [priestly] vestments, walls and panels, in houses and on streets, namely such images of Our Lord Jesus Christ . . . [the] Holy Mother of God, and of the honorable angels . . . and saints . . ." (*Definition of the Sacred Images and Tradition*, Action VII; cf. also CCC 1161).

Over seven hundred years later, the Council of Trent echoed the teachings of this council when it proclaimed dogmatically:

"The holy Synod enjoins on all bishops, and others who sustain the office and charge of teaching, that, agreeably to the usage of the Catholic and Apostolic Church, received from the primitive times of the Christian religion, and agreeably to the consent of the holy Fathers, and to the decrees of sacred Councils, they especially instruct the faithful diligently concerning the intercession and invocation of saints; the honor [paid] to relics; and the legitimate use of images: teaching them, that the saints, who reign together with Christ, offer up their own prayers to God for men; that it is good and useful suppliantly to invoke them, and to have recourse to their prayers, aid, [and] help for obtaining benefits from God, through His Son, Jesus Christ our Lord, who is alone our Redeemer and Savior; but that they think impiously, who deny that the saints, who enjoy eternal happiness in heaven, are to be invocated; or who assert either that they do not pray for men; or, that the invocation of them to pray for each of us even in particular, is idolatry; or, that it is repugnant to the word of God; and is opposed to the honor of the one mediator of God and men, Christ Jesus; or, that it is foolish to supplicate, vocally or mentally, those who reign in heaven. Also, that the holy bodies of holy martyrs, and of others now living with Christ, — which bodies were the living members of Christ, and the temple of the Holy Ghost, and which are by Him to be raised unto eternal life, and to be glorified, — are to be venerated by the faithful; through which [bodies] many benefits are bestowed by God on men; so that they who affirm that veneration and honor are not due to the relics of saints; or, that these, and other sacred monuments, are uselessly honored by the faithful; and that the places dedicated to the memories of the saints are in vain visited with the view of obtaining their aid; are wholly to be condemned, as the Church has already long since condemned, and now also condemns them" (Session 25, *Decree on the Invocation, Veneration, and Relics of Saints, and on Sacred Images*, 1563).

The council's teaching here sets forth a basic summary of the theological reasons why sacred images can be venerated, so long as there is no hint of idolatry. But also, we can't forget that the bishops who were assembled at the Council of Trent, as was the case with previous and subsequent deliberations by the magisterium on this subject, were keenly aware that the temptation to idolatry — icon worship, which is the grave sin of idolatry — is a perennial danger that stalks God's people (cf. Exodus 32). That's why the council Fathers added a lengthy and stringent warning about the proper use of sacred images so that the faithful would be better able to avoid the potential danger of the idolatry of icon worship:

> "Moreover, that the images of Christ, of the Virgin Mother of God, and of the other saints, are to be had and retained particularly in [churches], and that due honor and veneration are to be given them; not that any divinity, or virtue, is believed to be in them, on account of which they are to be worshipped; or that anything is to be asked of them; or, that trust is to be reposed in images, as was of old done by the Gentiles who placed their hope in idols; but because the honor which is shown them is referred to the prototypes which those images represent; in such wise that by the images which we kiss, and before which we uncover the head, and prostrate ourselves, we adore Christ; and we venerate the saints, whose likeness they bear: as, by the decrees of Councils, and especially of the second Synod of Nicaea, has been defined against the opponents of images.
>
> "And the bishops shall carefully teach this — that, by means of the histories of the mysteries of our Redemption, portrayed by paintings or other representations, the people is instructed, and confirmed in [the habit of] remembering, and continually revolving in mind the articles of faith; as also that great profit is derived from all sacred images, not only because the people are thereby admonished of the benefits and gifts bestowed upon them by Christ, but also because the miracles which God has performed by means of the saints, and

their salutary examples, are set before the eyes of the faithful; that so they may give God thanks for those things; may order their own lives and manners in imitation of the saints; and may be excited to adore and love God, and to cultivate piety. But if any one shall teach, or entertain sentiments, contrary to these decrees; let him be anathema.

"And if any abuses have crept in amongst these holy and salutary observances, the holy Synod ardently desires that they be utterly abolished; in such wise that no images, [suggestive] of false doctrine, and furnishing occasion of dangerous error to the uneducated, be set up. And if at times, when expedient for the unlettered people; it happen that the facts and narratives of sacred Scripture are portrayed and represented; the people shall be taught, that not thereby is the Divinity represented, as though it could be seen by the eyes of the body, or be portrayed by colors or figures.

"Moreover, in the invocation of saints, the veneration of relics, and the sacred use of images, every superstition shall be removed . . . let so great care and diligence be used herein by bishops, as that there be nothing seen that is disorderly, or that is unbecomingly or confusedly arranged, nothing that is profane, nothing indecorous, seeing that holiness becomes the house of God" (Session 25, *Decree on the Invocation, Veneration, and Relics of Saints, and on Sacred Images*, 1563).

Now that we've seen two examples of the Tradition of venerating the icons and other sacred images that depict Christ and the blessed in heaven, let's also look at other Christian testimony on the subject. First, though, keep in mind that in the first three centuries of the early Church there was a general (but by no means absolute) tendency to place no emphasis on icons. In fact, since Christianity sprang from Jewish roots, and since the Jews were keenly on guard against any form of idol-worship, it shouldn't surprise us that the earliest Christians largely ignored elaborate life-like icons or images, preferring instead to make do with their simple, symbolic icons[69] of fish, anchors, lambs, and shepherds.[70]

The practice of using icons and other sacred images, while uncommon at first, gradually became more widespread among Christians, so that once the Church was able to "come out of the catacombs" when the Roman laws prohibiting her were repealed under the Emperor Constantine in the early 300s, the practice began to become more widespread. Prior to that time we have evidence from a few Christian writers, such as St. Justin Martyr (100-165) and Athenagoras (second century), as well as from the regional synod of Elvira in Spain,[71] that among many Christians there was a tendency to avoid lifelike icons simply because they smacked of paganism and idol-worship, which they saw around them in all its hideous forms.

Indeed, we know that from at least the beginning of the second century, Christians became ever more prolific in their use of sacred images. Initially, they were simple and symbolic. Thousands of primitive Christian icons comprised of simple images are still extant throughout the catacombs in Rome[72] — bread in a basket (i.e., the Eucharist), a shepherd (Christ), a lamb (Christ), an anchor (Christ's faithfulness to his people), a vine (Christ and his followers), and of course the very popular fish symbol (Christ). The striking thing about these earliest sacred images was their simplicity. They showed through an analogy the theological truths they conveyed. Soon, more elaborate Christian icons were in use. There are many examples of icons of St. Peter and Christ together, sometimes with Christ ascending into heaven, and usually with Christ handing to Peter a scroll or keys, symbolizing the first pope's special authority given to him by the Lord (cf. Matthew 16:18–19).

All of these simple icons (i.e., frescoes, bas-relief carvings, as well as the more traditional form of icons that were painted on pieces of wood and were, therefore, portable) were in wide use among persecuted "underground" Christians, particularly in Rome and its environs, from the early second century onward. In addition to frescoes and the painted icons and Christian etchings in marble that adorn the galleries of the Roman catacombs, there are also any number of ossuaries (crypts) that bear the images of shepherds, fish, lambs, etc., again pointing to the use of sacred symbols and depictions of Christ among the early Christians.

And Mary had her place in the early tradition of sacred images. For example, there is also a remarkably well-preserved icon of the Blessed Virgin Mary holding the Christ Child in the catacombs of St. Priscilla in Rome. In this fresco we can see an Old Testament prophet standing to her side, holding a book (i.e., Scripture) and motioning with his arm to a star that hovers in space above Mary's head. Many scholars see in this simple Christian image an expression of two scriptural passages: Isaiah 60:19 and Numbers 24:17.

This sacred image of Christ and the Virgin Mary, painted and venerated by the early Christians, dates back to the second century, long before the Church was able to emerge from her long night of persecution by the Roman state in the fourth century. Some will argue that it was only then, only when Christianity was made legal by the Roman Emperor Constantine, that Christians began to make use of icons and sacred images. The argument entails the allegation that it was at this point in history that Christianity became corrupted by the influence of paganism, and that only then did the tradition of icons come into play. But this is completely incorrect and incompatible with the verifiable facts of history. The Christian tradition of making, using, and venerating sacred images well preceded the legalization of Christianity in the fourth century.

And perhaps most striking of all is that, Catholics and Orthodox aside, even many Evangelical and Fundamentalist Protestants have retained the ancient Christian tradition of using these simple icons, such as the "fish" symbol.

The Tradition of the Fish

Here's how and why this Christian tradition developed. The "fish" symbol was one of the very first — perhaps the first — sacred image to be popular among the early Christians. Its significance arose from a Greek acronym that signified a compact statement of faith. The first letter of each word of a Greek phrase — *Iesous Christos Huios Theou, Soter* ("Jesus Christ Son of God, Savior") — widely used among the early Christians spells out the Greek word for fish: *ichthus*, as it's transliterated into English. The *ichthus* symbol was a simple icon of Christ. And it's remarkable that Evangelical Protestants, the ones who so often rail against the Catholic tradition of sacred images, are themselves the willing heirs of this holy custom. You'll see proof of this on their cars (the fish symbol) on their clothing (fish symbol lapel pins), on business cards, signs, T-shirts, and all manner of other places Christians can place that symbol. Now, as in the early Church, the fish symbol is a code that means one thing: Jesus Christ. You will not see Muslims or Hindus or

Buddhists sporting fish lapel pins. They know the meaning of that icon and who it represents.

Eventually, the fish symbol gave way to the crucifix. Once the first several generations of Christians had passed, the immediate, living memory of the horror that was death by Roman crucifixion began to fade. The pathos and depth of meaning of the crucifixion was ever present in the minds of the early Christians, of course; but once the Church emerged from its long night of persecution in the catacombs, the practice of imaging the Lord Jesus on the cross became more and more popular. At first, simple representations of the cross were quite common, and before long the corpus was shown on the cross, depicting the Lord's ultimate sacrifice and victory. The Christian tradition of the crucifix gained ascendancy in sacred art not long after the Emperor Constantine lifted the ban on Christianity and the Church was free to develop her own sacred art.

The crucifix was a traditional way for Christians to live out the words of St. Paul: "For I decided to know nothing among you except Jesus Christ and him crucified" (1 Corinthians 2:2; cf. 1 Corinthians 1:17-18). The late, great Archbishop Fulton Sheen gave us a marvelous reminder of the importance of the crucifix: "Keep your eyes on the crucifix; for Jesus without the cross is a man without a mission, and the cross without Jesus is a burden without a reliever."

And that bit of wisdom brings us back to the essential purpose of crucifixes, statues, icons, and sacred images: They serve to remind us of our heroes in the Faith, Jesus Christ, the Blessed Virgin Mary, and all the saints. These images are symbols in wood or stone, plaster or paint, physical depictions that help enable the human mind to better grasp unseen realities. We humans rely on these kinds of "visual aids" to remind us of things and people we can't see or touch physically, not because we invest some sort of intrinsic value in the paint or piece of wood or hunk of marble that becomes the sacred image, but rather we see past the physical depiction to the reality it represents.

This is a universal human circumstance, shown by the fact that people everywhere have photographs of loved ones. I, for example, carry pictures of my wife and children with me when I travel. If someone were to see me happen to kiss the picture of my family at a moment when I was far from them and missed them, that person wouldn't be shocked and wouldn't assume that I loved the Kodak paper on which their images are depicted!

If we examine the evidence, we'll soon discover that the theology of the icon was deeply embedded in the teaching, worship, and evangelization efforts of the early Christians. Their purpose, then as now, was to convey doctrinal truths through the medium of symbols; to depict the reality of certain key historical events important to Christians (such as martyrdoms and Christ conferring authority on Peter), as well as to express through these images the truths of the Christian Faith.

While always maintaining a careful balance between the sin of idolatry (a constant danger Christians must guard against) and the true and good practice of giving authentic respect and veneration to icons, the Fathers of the Church we'll briefly survey here remind us of the importance of sacred images in the life of the Church.

St. Basil the Great,[73] A.D. 329–379 — "Rise now before me, you painters of the saints' merits, complete with your art this incomplete image of a great leader [i.e., to complete with their icons of St. Barlaam what Basil left 'unfinished' with his words]. Illuminate with the flowers of your wisdom the indistinct image of which I have drawn [i.e., verbally] of the crowned martyr. Let my words be surpassed by your painting of the heroic deeds of the martyr. . . . I will look at this fighter represented in a more living way on your paintings. Let the demons cry, once again defeated by the courage of the martyr! . . . And let the Initiator of combats, Christ, also be represented in this painting" (*Oration* 17). In that stirring message from the great bishop, we see the thrust of the Church's tradition on icons: their value is not in their beauty but in their power to teach, to communicate through art the valiant sufferings of the martyrs, and the bigger picture of the Gospel as a whole.

Orthodox scholar Leonid Ouspensky offers an important observation regarding the nature of icons and how utterly different they are from idols:

> "What primarily amazes a believer, Orthodox and Catholic, is the confusion between an idol and a Christian image. We know that, in fact, the Church, throughout its history, drew a very clear line between the two. The proofs of this are not lacking in the works of the writers of antiquity, nor in the lives of the saints of the first centuries, nor in the *Ecclesiastical History* of Eusebius [circa A.D. 260-341], nor in later sources. When, for example, pagan Russia was converted to Christianity [in the ninth and tenth centuries], the first thing St. Vladimir did was to destroy the idols and to propagate icons."[74]

That insightful comment is an echo of the constant teaching of the Church herself: "Idolatry not only refers to false pagan worship. It remains a constant temptation to faith. Idolatry consists in divinizing what is not God. Man commits idolatry whenever he honors and reveres a creature in place of God, whether this be gods or demons (for example, satanism), power, pleasure, race, ancestors, the state, money, etc. Jesus says, 'You cannot serve God and mammon' [Matthew 6:24]. Many martyrs died for not adoring 'the Beast' [cf. Revelation 13:14], refusing even to simulate such worship. Idolatry rejects the unique Lordship of God; it is therefore incompatible with communion with God [cf. Galatians 5:20; Ephesians 5:5]" (CCC 2113).

This Tradition was echoed by the Church in later centuries by statements such as these:

St. Basil the Great, A.D. 329–379 — "[T]he honor paid to the image [i.e., icons] passes on to the prototype [i.e., the Lord, or the saint represented by the icon]. Now what in the one case the image is by reason of imitation, that in the other case the Son is by nature; and as in works of art the likeness is dependent on the form, so in the case of the divine and uncompounded nature the union consists in the communion of the Godhead" (*On the Holy Spirit* 18:45).

Theodore the Reader of Constantinople, circa A.D. **530** — This Eastern Catholic historian wrote at length about the long-standing tradition that St. Luke himself painted the first icons of Our Lady and the Christ Child. This tradition about St. Luke and icons was well attested to in the Eastern Church, and many accounts say that St. Luke gave these icons to the "Most Excellent Theophilus," to whom he dedicated his Gospel and the Book of Acts (cf. Luke 1:3-4; Acts 1:1).

The Council of Constantinople IV, A.D. **869-870** — "We decree that the sacred image of our lord Jesus Christ, the redeemer and savior of all people, should be venerated with honor equal to that given to the book of the holy gospels. For, just as through the written words which are contained in the book, we all shall obtain salvation, so through the influence that colors in painting exercise on the imagination, all, both wise and simple, obtain benefit from what is before them; for as speech teaches and portrays through syllables, so too does painting by means of colors. It is only right then, in accordance with true reason and very ancient tradition, that icons should be honored and venerated in a derivative way because of the honor which is given to their archetypes, and it should be equal to that given to the sacred book of the holy gospels and the representation of the precious cross" (canon 3).

18. The Veneration of Relics

In my book on the communion of saints, *Any Friend of God's Is a Friend of Mine* (Basilica Press, 1996), I explain the rise of the ancient Christian practice of venerating the relics of departed Christians known for their sanctity and love for Jesus Christ, especially those of the martyrs:

"The early Church's keen awareness of the communion of saints was rooted in its veneration of the many martyrs, victims of Roman persecution in the first few centuries after Christ. The early Christians' love for their slain brethren was manifested in the liturgies, hymns, prayers, and writings of the Fathers and Doctors. Masses were celebrated in honor of the martyrs. Mosaics depicting their lives and martyrdoms adorned countless ancient churches." [75]

Their intercession was universally invoked by the early Church. Their relics were safeguarded and venerated, and the moving accounts of their heroic deaths for Christ were carefully preserved, copied, and disseminated among the churches everywhere. The Church's theology of the communion of saints developed rapidly, and patristic writings that explain and emphasize the Church's honoring of the saints and reliance upon their heavenly intercession abound.

The late Church historian Henri Daniel-Rops describes this aspect of the early Church:

> "The martyrs tended in every respect to disrupt Roman authority, simply by their patient suffering and their serene acceptance of self-sacrifice. . . On the other hand, it need hardly be said that for their brethren in Christ their oblation had an exemplary value whose importance cannot be overestimated. Heroism has an appeal which is well known to anyone who has fought in a war and led men into battle. From the very first moment that the Roman state had begun to attack the Christians, it had put this powerful weapon of propaganda into their hands. The more public and widespread it made its persecutions, the more it worked to further that spread of the faith, through the blood of the martyrs, of which Tertullian had spoken."[76]

The martyrs triumphed mightily through their steadfast faith in Christ, a courageous faith that preferred the pains of a cruel death to the alternative of renouncing the Lord in order to escape their persecutors. Their triumph was not only in their winning the glorious prize of eternal life that waited for them in heaven (cf. Hebrews 11:32-39; 12:1-11); they also defeated the agents of the powers of death by showing, through their willingness to sacrifice their own earthly lives, that the life-giving Resurrection of Christ conquers death in the end.

One Catholic historian examining the panorama of early Christian history described the volume of evidence for the Tradition of venerating Christian relics in this way: "From the Catholic standpoint there was no extravagance or abuse in this cult [i.e., the Christian practice of venerating relics] as it was recommended and indeed taken for granted, by writers like St. Augustine, St. Ambrose, St. Jerome, St. Gregory of Nyssa, St. [John] Chrysostom, St. Gregory Nazianzen, and by all the other great doctors without exception."[77]

The early Church Fathers testify that this was the authentic tradition in the ancient Church. They knew well this truth: "Precious in the eyes of the Lord is the death of his saints" (Psalm 116:15). Since they knew that the body of a Christian is the "temple of the Holy Spirit" (1 Corinthians 6:19), they were especially concerned with showing the respect, even veneration, for the relics of the martyrs.

The Church at Smyrna, circa A.D. 156 — "[After the martyrdom of Polycarp] we took up his bones, as being more precious than the most exquisite jewels, and more purified than gold, and deposited them in a fitting place, whither, being gathered together, as opportunity is allowed us, with joy and rejoicing, the Lord shall grant us to celebrate the anniversary of his martyrdom, both in memory of those who have already finished their course, and for the exercising and preparation of those yet to walk in their steps" (*The Martyrdom of Polycarp* 18).

St. Ambrose of Milan, circa A.D. 388 — "As I do not wish anything which takes place here in your absence to escape the knowledge of your holiness [i.e., referring to his sister, to whom he was writing], you must know that we have found some bodies of holy martyrs [Gervasius and Protasius]. For after I had dedicated the basilica, many, as it were, with one mouth began to address me, and said, 'Consecrate this as you did the Roman basilica.' And I answered, 'Certainly I will if I find any relics of martyrs.' And at once a kind of prophetic ardor seemed to enter my heart. . . .

"I found the fitting signs, and on bringing in some on whom hands were to be laid, the power of the holy martyrs became so manifest, that even whilst I was still silent, one was seized and thrown prostrate at the holy burial-place. We found two men of marvelous stature, such as those of ancient days. All the bones were perfect, and there was much blood. During the whole of those two days there was an enormous concourse of people. Briefly we arranged the whole in order, and as evening was now coming on transferred them to the basilica of Fausta, where watch was kept during the night, and some received the laying on of hands. On the following day we translated the relics to the basilica called Ambrosian. During the translation [i.e., the transfer of the relics] a blind man was healed. I addressed the people then as follows:

"When I considered the immense and unprecedented numbers of you who are here gathered together, and the gifts of divine grace which have shone forth in the holy martyrs, I must confess that I felt myself unequal to this task, and that I could not express in words what we can scarcely conceive in our minds or take in with our eyes. But when the course of holy Scripture began to be read, the Holy Spirit Who spake in the prophets granted me to utter something worthy of so great a gathering, of your expectations, and of the merits of the holy martyrs.

" 'The heavens,' it is said, 'declare the glory of God.' When this Psalm is read, it occurs to one that not so much the material elements as the heavenly merits seem to offer praise worthy of God. And by the chance of this day's lessons it is made clear what 'heavens' declare the glory of God. Look at the holy relics at my right hand and at my left, see men of heavenly conversation, behold the trophies of a heavenly mind. These are the heavens which declare the glory of God, these are His handiwork which the firmament proclaims. For not worldly enticements, but the grace of the divine working, raised them to the firmament of the most sacred Passion, and long before by the testimony of their character and virtues bore witness of them, that they continued steadfast against the dangers of this world. . . .

"For not without reason do many call this the resurrection of the martyrs. I do not say whether they have risen for themselves, for us certainly the martyrs have risen. You know — nay, you have yourselves seen — that many are cleansed from evil spirits, that very many also, having touched with their hands the robe of the saints, are freed from those ailments which oppressed them; you see that the miracles of old time are renewed, when through the coming of the Lord Jesus grace was more largely shed forth upon the earth, and that many bodies are healed as it were by the shadow of the holy bodies. How many napkins are passed about! how many garments, laid upon the holy relics and endowed with healing power, are claimed! All are glad to touch even the outside thread, and whosoever touches will be made whole. . . .

"Thanks be to Thee, Lord Jesus, that at this time Thou hast stirred up for us the spirits of the holy martyrs, when Thy Church needs greater protection. Let all know what sort of champions [i.e., martyrs] I desire, who are able to defend, but desire not to attack. These have I gained for you, O holy people, such as may help all and injure none. Such defenders do I desire, such are the soldiers I have, that is, not soldiers of this world, but soldiers of Christ. I fear no ill-will on account of them, the more powerful their patronage is, the greater safety is there in it. And I wish for their protection for those very persons who grudge them to me. Let them come, then, and see my attendants. I do not deny that I am surrounded by such arms: 'Some trust in chariots, and some in horses, but we will boast in the Name of the Lord our God' " (*Epistle 22*).

St. Cyril of Jerusalem, circa A.D. 350 — "[E]ven though the soul is not present [in the body, i.e., after death], a virtue resides in the body of the saints, because of the righteous soul which has for so many years dwelled in it, and used it as its minister. And let us not foolishly disbelieve, as though this thing had not happened: for if handkerchiefs and aprons [cf. Acts 5:15; 19:11-12], which are from without, touching the bodies of the diseased, raised up the sick, how much more should the very body of the Prophet [Elisha] raise the dead?[78] [cf. 2 Kings 13:21; Sirach 48:14]" (*Catechetical Lectures*).

St. Augustine of Hippo, inter A.D. 413-426 — "This I might say for the sake of refuting these most frivolous objectors. But we cannot deny that many miracles were wrought to confirm that one grand and health-giving miracle of Christ's ascension to heaven with the flesh in which He rose. For these most trustworthy books of ours contain in one narrative both the miracles that were wrought and the creed which they were wrought to confirm. The miracles were published that they might produce faith, and the faith which they produced brought them into greater prominence. For they are read in congregations that they may be believed, and yet they would not be so read unless they were believed. For even now miracles are wrought in the name of Christ, whether by His sacraments or by the prayers or relics of His saints" (*City of God* 22:8).

St. Jerome, circa A.D. 400 — "We do not worship, we do not adore [Latin: *non colimus, non adoramus*], for fear that we should bow down to the creature rather than to the Creator, but we venerate [Latin: *honoramus*] the relics of the martyrs in order the better to adore Him whose martyrs they are" (*To Riparius*).

---

19. The Name 'Catholic' for the Original Christian Church

The formal or official name for the Church established by Jesus Christ is the Catholic Church. Its use in the early Church among the Fathers and Doctors (as in later centuries) was to distinguish the one, true Church established by Jesus Christ from all other groups, including those heretical or aberrant groups that claimed the name "Catholic."

Perhaps the best place to start with examples of Tradition and why we have them is the very name of the Church Christ established on the rock of Peter: the Catholic Church. This subject may not at first seem necessary to spend much time on, but I believe it's worth examining at some depth, getting a sense of what the early Church meant by this tradition of calling the Church "catholic." By spending extra time and space studying this core tradition, we will be much better equipped to understand the origin and purpose of the other "capital-T" Traditions and "small-t" traditions we'll encounter later in this book. To put it another way, only after we understand how the early Christians understood the nature and identity of the Church — the Catholic Church — only then can we better appreciate why that ancient Church taught her particular doctrines and adopted her many customs and disciplines.

Many people bandy about the factoid that "catholic" means "universal," and it does, but that's not all it means. Our English word "catholic" derives from a

Greek compound word, *katholokos*, which is related to the Greek term *katholou* (*kathos* + *holos*), which literally means "for the whole." It is truly in this sense that we can see the meaning of the word "Catholic" and how it came to be applied as the formal name of the Church established by Christ, even in the very earliest years of Christianity.

The origin of this ancient Christian practice of calling the Church "Catholic" is not clear, but we do know for sure that it was already in use by the year 107. St. Ignatius of Antioch, a successor bishop to St. Peter in that city, said this in one of his famous letters, which he penned as he was being escorted under guard to Rome, where he would be martyred:

"See that you all follow the bishop, even as Jesus Christ does [follow] the Father, and the presbytery as you would the apostles; and reverence the deacons, as being the institution of God. Let no man do anything connected with the Church without the bishop. Let that be deemed a proper Eucharist, which is [celebrated] either by the bishop, or by one to whom he has entrusted it. Wherever the bishop shall appear, there let the multitude [i.e., the faithful] also be; even as, wherever Jesus Christ is, there is the Catholic Church" (*Epistle to the Smyrneans* 8).

It's interesting that St. Ignatius' reference to "the Catholic Church" wasn't questioned or queried by other Christian writers of his day or in years to come. It seems clear that his use of the term "Catholic" was reflective of a tradition already in usage among the early Christians. Other monuments of this tradition are *The Letter on the Martyrdom of Polycarp*, written by the Church at Smyrna (section 16, A.D. 107).

Clement of Alexandria said, "We say that both in substance and in seeming, both in origin and in development, the primitive and Catholic Church is the only one, agreeing as it does in the unity of one faith" (*Stromata* 7:16).

And in the early Church, the term Catholic was, if you'll excuse the pun, universally recognized as the title for the Christian Church. Repeatedly, the Fathers and Doctors of the Church, including those from the beginning of the second century, refer to the "Catholic Church" and by that term meant the specific Church we know of today as Catholic, complete with a pope, sacraments, and the body of doctrines unique to herself and distinguishable from all the sects and heretical groups that squabbled among themselves and competed for the title "the Church."

An example of this fact comes from St. Augustine of Hippo, who delivered a scathing rebuke to Petilianus, a heretical teacher in his day whom he corresponded with in an attempt to bring him home to the Church.[79] In a few places, St. Augustine slammed Petilianus's attempts to characterize his heretical sect as "Catholic," saying he didn't know whether to laugh or cry at the other man's efforts to cloak his errors under the title "Catholic."

Augustine begins his argument by mentioning that "Petilianus said: 'If you declare that you hold the Catholic Church, the word "catholic" is merely the Greek equivalent for entire or whole. But it is clear that you are not in the whole, because you have gone aside into the part.'

"I too indeed have attained to a very slight knowledge of the Greek language," St. Augustine continues, "scarcely to be called knowledge at all, yet I am not shameless in saying that I know that [the Greek word] *holon* means not 'one,' but 'the whole;' and that [the Greek compound word] *kath-holon* means 'according to the whole' — whence the Catholic Church received its name, according to the saying of the Lord,

'It is not for you to know the times, which the Father hath put in His own power. But you shall receive power, after that the Holy Ghost will come upon you: and you shall be witnesses unto me both in Jerusalem, and in Judea, and in Samaria, and even in the whole earth' [Acts 1:7-8]. Here you have the origin of the name 'Catholic.' But you are so bent upon running with your eyes shut against the mountain which grew out of a small stone [i.e., the Catholic Church; cf. Matthew 16:18-19], according to the prophecy of Daniel, and filled the whole earth [cf. Daniel 2:35], that you actually tell us that we have gone aside into a part [i.e., into schism as a splinter group], and are not in the whole among those whose communion is spread throughout the whole earth. But just in the same way as, supposing you were to say that I [Augustine] was Petilianus, I should not be able to find any method of refuting you unless I were to laugh at you as being in jest, or mourn over you as being insane, so in the present case I see that I have no other choice but this; and since I do not believe that you are in jest, you see what alternative remains."[80]

As in the early Church, even today many want to deny that the name "Catholic" refers to (or should refer to) a specific Church, the Church of Rome. They will argue that the use of the term "Catholic" in the creeds and early Christian writings should always be understood in a "small-c" sense, not in a "capital-C" sense that would connote the meaning of a specific Church — the Catholic Church. Some, including some Reformed Protestants, seek to establish that they, too, are "catholic," at least in the sense that they claim to be of the same religion as the "catholic Church" spoken about in the Nicene Creed. But they are mistaken. Many of these same people will argue, oddly, that the Catholic Church — the *Roman* Catholic

Church, as they like to emphasize — cannot be the same "catholic Church" referred to in the Creed. It's a bizarre line of reasoning and illogic that would allow for just about any Protestant group to shelter under the title "Catholic" and, at the same time, deny that title to the Catholic Church, which can, unlike the Protestant groups, trace her existence and her peculiarly "catholic" teachings back to the early Church!

One Evangelical Protestant apologist once claimed in a letter to me that the Catholic Church isn't really catholic. "After all," he argued, "if it's 'Roman,' it cannot be catholic, and if it's 'catholic,' it cannot be Roman." (One can imagine how St. Augustine would have rolled his eyes in exasperation after reading that tortured reasoning.) The fact is, the moniker "Roman Catholic" is actually a term imposed on Catholics from the outside, stemming mainly from Anglican efforts in past centuries to portray themselves as also truly Catholic, their claim being that there are three "branches" of the Catholic Church: the Orthodox, "Roman" Catholic, and Anglican. But this argument is not true and it clashes completely with how the early Christians understood their use of the word "Catholic."

St. Augustine again forcefully explained what the early Christians meant by the term "Catholic." We can see clearly that the early Christian tradition of referring to the Church as the Catholic Church was rooted in her belief that she alone preserved in her integrity the teachings of Christ and the Apostles:

"We must hold to the Christian religion and to communication in her Church, which is Catholic and which is called Catholic not only by her own members but even by all her enemies. For when heretics or the adherents of schisms talk about her, not among themselves but with strangers, willy-nilly, they call her nothing else but Catholic. For they will not be understood unless they distinguish her by this name which the whole world employs in her regard" (*On the True Religion* 7:12, A.D. 390).

"We believe in the 'holy catholic Church,' that is, the Catholic Church; for heretics violate the Faith itself by a false opinion about God; schismatics, however, withdraw from a fraternal love by hostile separations, although they believe the same things we do. Consequently, neither heretics nor schismatics belong to the Catholic Church" (*Faith and Creed* 10:21, A.D. 393).

"In the Catholic Church . . . there are many things which can most properly keep me in her bosom. The unanimity of peoples and nations keeps me here. Her authority, inaugurated in miracles, nourished by hope, augmented by love, and confirmed by her age, keeps me here. The succession of priests, from the very See of Apostle Peter [i.e., from Rome, the location of the pope, the successor of St. Peter], to whom the Lord, after his Resurrection, gave the charge of feeding his sheep [cf. John 21:15-18], up to the present episcopate [of the bishop of Rome at that time], keeps me here. And last, the very name 'Catholic,' which, not without reason, belongs to this Church alone, in the face of so many heretics, so much so that, though all heretics want to be called 'Catholic,' when a stranger inquires where the Catholic Church meets, none of the heretics would dare to point out his own basilica or house" (*Against the Letter of Mani Called 'The Foundation'* 4:5, A.D. 397).

The early councils (e.g., Nicaea I, A.D. 325, Constantinople I, A.D. 381, and Chalcedon, A.D. 451) frequently referred to the Church as the "Catholic Church," vociferously defending and equating orthodox Christian teaching with adherence to the teaching of the Catholic Church. Other notable examples of the early Christians defining what they meant by the term "Catholic,"[81] as well as the antiquity of its usage, are:

St. Clement of Alexandria, A.D. 207 — "From what has been said, then, it is my opinion that the true Church, that which is really ancient, is one, and that in it those who according to God's purpose are just, are enrolled. For from the very reason that God is one, and the Lord one, that which is in the highest degree honorable is lauded in consequence of its singleness, being an imitation of the one first principle. In the nature of the One, then, is associated in a joint heritage the one Church, which they strive to cut asunder into many sects. Therefore in substance and idea, in origin, in pre-eminence, we say that the ancient and Catholic Church is alone . . ." (*Stromata* 7:17).

St. Cyprian of Carthage, A.D. 254 — "They vainly flatter themselves who creep up, not having peace with the priests of God [i.e., not in communion with the magisterium of the Church] believing that they are secretly in communion with certain individuals. For the Church, which is one and Catholic, is not split or divided, but it is indeed united and joined by the cement of [the] priests who adhere to one another" (Letter 68, *To Florentius, On Calumniators* 8).

St. Cyril of Jerusalem, circa A.D. 347 — "[The Church] is called Catholic, then, because it extends over the whole world, from end to end of the earth, and because it teaches universally and infallibly each and every doctrine which must come to the knowledge of men concerning things visible and invisible . . . because it universally treats and heals every class of sins, those committed with the soul and those with the body, and it possesses within itself every conceivable form of virtue, in deeds and in words and in the spiritual gifts of every description" (*Catechetical Lectures* 18:23, 18:26).

St. Vincent of Lerins, A.D. 434 — "I have often then inquired earnestly and attentively of very many men eminent for sanctity and learning, how and by what sure and so to speak universal rule I may be able to distinguish the truth of Catholic faith from the falsehood of heretical depravity; and I have always, and in almost every instance, received an answer to this effect: That whether I or any one else should wish to detect the frauds and avoid the snares of heretics as they rise, and to continue sound and complete in the Catholic faith, we must, the Lord helping, fortify our own belief in two ways; first, by the authority of the Divine Law, and then, by the Tradition of the Catholic Church" (*Commonotoria* 2:1-2).

20. Calling Priests 'Father'

This traditional Catholic practice makes many Protestants' hair stand on end. They believe that Catholics, who call priests "father," blatantly violate Christ's prohibition in Scripture, "Call no man 'father' " (cf. Matthew 23:9). In my book *Where Is That in the Bible?* I provide you with many biblical citations Catholics can use to demonstrate that this Catholic practice is not a violation of the Lord's command; rather, we can summarize those biblical evidences this way: Christ's intention was to steer us away from looking to any human being as if he was our father in the way only God is our Father. His intention was *not* to prohibit us from literally referring to priests as "father," and we can prove that by the fact that, while under the inspiration of the Holy Spirit, St. Stephen publicly addressed the Jewish leaders as "my brothers and fathers" (cf. Acts 7:2). St. Paul also added that "though you have countless guides in Christ, you do not have many fathers. For I became your father in Christ Jesus through the gospel. I urge you, then, be imitators of me" (1 Corinthians 4:15-16, RSV).

This understanding of that Gospel passage was clear in the early Church. The custom of calling bishops and priests "father" arose very early. Even the custom of calling the bishop of Rome "pope" derives from the affectionate Latin word for "father": *papa*.

St. Irenaeus of Lyons, circa A.D. 180 — "Since, therefore, all things were made by God, and since the devil has become the cause of apostasy to himself and others, justly does the Scripture always term those who remain in a state of apostasy 'sons of the devil'[82] and 'angels of the wicked one.' For [the word] 'son,' as one before me has observed, has a twofold meaning: one [is a son] in the order of nature, because he was born a son; the other, in that he was made so, is reputed a son, although there be a difference between being born so and being made so. For the first is indeed born from the person referred to; but the second is made so by him, whether as respects his creation or by the teaching of his doctrine. *For when any person has been taught from the mouth of another, he is termed the son of him who instructs him, and the latter [is called] his father*" (*Against All Heresies* 4:41:2; emphasis mine).

St. Clement of Alexandria, circa A.D. 202 — "[H]e who proclaims the truth is to be prevented from leaving behind him what is to benefit posterity. It is a good thing, I reckon, to leave good children to posterity. This is the case with children of our bodies. But words are the progeny of the soul. Hence we call those who have instructed us, fathers" (*Miscellanies* 1:1).

Flavian, Bishop of Constantinople, circa A.D. 445 — "To the most holy and God-loving father and fellow-bishop, Leo, Flavian greeting in the Lord! There is nothing which can stay the devil's wickedness, that 'restless evil, full of deadly poison.'[83] Above and below it 'goes about,' seeking 'whom it may' strike, dismay, and 'devour.'[84] Whence to watch, to be sober unto prayer, to draw near to God, to eschew foolish questionings, *to follow the fathers* and not to go beyond the eternal bounds, this we have learnt from Holy Writ. And so I give up the excess of grief and abundant tears over the capture of one of the clergy who are under me, and whom I could not save nor snatch from the wolf, although I was ready to lay down my life for him. How was he caught, how did he leap away, hating the voice of the caller *and turning aside also from the memory of the fathers*[85] and thoroughly detesting their paths? And thus I proceed with my account" (*First Letter to Pope Leo the Great*; emphasis mine).

Theodoret, Bishop of Cyrus, circa A.D. 449 — "First of all, I beg you to tell me, whether I ought to acquiesce in this unrighteous deposition or not. For I await your verdict and, if you bid me abide by my condemnation, I will abide by it, and will trouble no one hereafter, but await the unerring verdict of our God and Savior. . . . And before all things I entreat you, holy and God-loved brother, render assistance to my prayers. These things I have brought to your Holiness' knowledge, by the most religious and God-beloved presbyters, Hypatius and Abramius . . . and Alypius, superintendent of the monks in our district: seeing that I was hindered from coming to you myself by the Emperor's restraining letter, and likewise the others. And I entreat your holiness both to *look on them with fatherly regard*, and to lend them your ears in sincere kindness, and also to deem my slandered and falsely attacked position worthy of your protection, and above all to defend with all your might the Faith that is now plotted against, and to *keep the heritage of the fathers intact for the churches*, so shall your holiness receive from the Bountiful Master a full reward" (*Letter to Pope Leo the Great*; emphasis mine).

This next example not only shows the strong tradition of calling bishops (and the pope) "father," it also points out the primacy of the bishop of Rome in matters of teaching. Here we see three bishops from what is now France (Gaul) writing to the bishop of Rome, Leo, thanking him for his instructions and asking him for clarification on certain other points.

Three Bishops of Gaul, circa A.D. 450 — "Ceretius, Salonius and Veranus to the holy Lord, most blessed father, and pope most worthy of the Apostolic See, Leo. . . . Having perused your Excellency's letter, which you composed for instruction in the Faith, and sent to the bishop of Constantinople, we thought it our duty, being enriched with so great a wealth of doctrine, to pay our debt of thanks by at least [responding to you with] a letter. For we appreciate your fatherly solicitude on our behalf, and confess that we are the more indebted to your preventing care because we now have the benefit of the remedy before experiencing the evils. For knowing that those remedies are well-nigh too late which are applied after the infliction of the wounds, you admonish us with the voice of loving forethought to arm ourselves with those Apostolic means of defense. We acknowledge frankly, most blessed pope, with what singular loving-kindness you have imparted to us the innermost thoughts of your breast, by the efficacy of which you secure the safety of others: and while you extract the old Serpent's infused poison from the hearts of others, standing as it were on the watch-tower of Love, with Apostolic care and watchfulness you cry aloud, lest the enemy come on us unawares and off our guard, lest careless security expose us to attack, O holy Lord, most blessed father and pope, most worthy of the Apostolic See. Moreover we, who specially belong to you, are filled with a great and unspeakable delight, because this special statement of your teaching is so highly regarded wherever the Churches meet together, that the unanimous opinion is expressed that the primacy of the Apostolic See is rightfully there assigned, from whence the oracles of the Apostolic Spirit still receive their interpretations" (*Epistle to Pope Leo the Great*).

---

21. Holy Water

This Catholic tradition is particularly beautiful and rich in meaning, and it's also of very early origin in the life of the Church. The primary meaning of this ancient custom is to signify the baptismal "washing of the soul" that takes place at baptism. As St. Paul explains: "[H]e saved us through the bath of rebirth / and renewal by the holy Spirit, / whom he richly poured out on us / through Jesus Christ our savior, / so that we might be justified by his grace / and become heirs in hope of eternal life" (Titus 3:5-7, NAB). Each time a Catholic enters a church and dips his hand into the holy water font to bless himself with the sign of the cross, he is renewing his baptismal covenant with God. This grace-filled action recalls the words of St. Paul above as well as reminds us of our baptism "in the name of the Father and of the Son and of the Holy Spirit" (Matthew 28:19, RSV).

St. Gregory Nazianzus, one of the major early Church Fathers, said, "Through Baptism the Christian is sacramentally assimilated to Jesus, who in his own baptism anticipates his death and resurrection.

The Christian must enter into this mystery of humble self-abasement and repentance, go down into the water with Jesus in order to rise with him, be reborn of water and the Spirit so as to become the Father's beloved son in the Son and 'walk in newness of life' [Romans 6:4]. Let us be buried with Christ by baptism to rise with him; let us go down with him to be raised with him; and let us rise with him to be glorified with him" (*Oratio* 40, 9; cf. CCC 537).

And as with all Christian customs and traditions, the tradition of using holy water can be misunderstood and even abused. The first thing to remember is that holy water is not "magic." It is not in itself anything remarkable. Rather, what makes holy water a sacred element is the grace and love of God himself who, through the action of the priest who blesses ordinary water, endows it with special dignity precisely because now that water has the particular blessing and signification of the salvific work Christ accomplished on the cross and which he "pours out" on us through baptism. That's why it's good and proper for Catholics to not only bless themselves with holy water but to bless their homes and their children with it. The grace of God can be communicated to us through tangible, physical elements such as bread and wine (cf. 1 Corinthians 10:16).

We have evidence that this practice was widespread among Christians as early as the fourth century. For example, the holy **Bishop Epiphanius of Salamis** (A.D. 310-403) described the blessing of water by the priest or bishop by uttering a prayer and "making over the vessel with his finger the seal of the cross" (cf. *Against All Heresies* 30:12). He even recounts the story of a holy layman named Joseph who sprinkled holy water on a possessed person and commanded: "In the name of Jesus Christ of Nazareth, crucified, depart from this unhappy one, thou infernal spirit, and let him be healed!"

Just as the Lord Jesus used water (spittle) mixed with clay to form mud with which he healed a man blind from birth (cf. John 9:16), he also uses water and other humble elements (e.g., bread, wine, oil) to impart his grace. The Catholic Church's tradition of using holy water to bless people, places, and things, is a direct result of her understanding of the Tradition of baptismal regeneration. That Tradition is the doctrinal foundation for the tradition of holy water.

22. Sacramentals

Sacramentals are sacred signs, elements, and gestures that impart graces instituted by the Church that help us become better disposed to receive the sacraments and to draw near to Christ. They also symbolize the realities of the sacraments, much the way a wedding ring symbolizes the reality of marriage. In itself, the ring is simply a sign, a symbol of something else. The same is true of sacramentals. Things like medals, holy cards, scapulars, holy water, and the like are sacred insofar as they represent sacred realities, but there is no inherent quality of the object itself that goes beyond the symbolic.

The *Catechism* explains the nature and purpose of the tradition of sacramentals: "Sacramentals are instituted for the sanctification of certain ministries of the Church, certain states of life, a great variety of circumstances in Christian life, and the use of many things helpful to man. In accordance with bishops' pastoral decisions, they can also respond to the needs, culture, and special history of the Christian people of a particular region or time. They always include a prayer, often accompanied by a specific sign, such as the laying on of hands, the sign of the cross, or the sprinkling of holy water (which recalls Baptism)" (CCC 1668).

Unlike the sacraments, which were instituted by Christ, sacramentals were instituted by the Church. They are "sacred signs which bear a resemblance to the sacraments. They signify effects, particularly of a spiritual nature, which are obtained through the intercession of the Church. By them men are disposed to receive the chief effect of the sacraments, and various occasions in life are rendered holy" (*Sacrosanctum Concilium* 60).

Common examples of sacramentals are blessings, making the sign of the cross, the veneration of relics, holy water, statues, medals, the scapular, the rosary, prayerful reading of Scripture, the ceremonial gestures and signs found in the Church's liturgies (e.g., the "orans" prayer position), the rites of administering the sacraments, pilgrimages, votive candles, incense, processions, almsgiving, the blessing from a priest or bishop, blessings with chrism (oil), and crucifixes.

The earliest references to sacramentals deal mainly with the rites of administering the sacraments. Later, as the theology of sacramentals developed and their use became more widespread in Catholic piety, the statements from early Church sources become broader, encompassing more things. The longer quote from St. Basil (see below) is very important in understanding why sacramentals are part of Christian tradition. Read it carefully and prayerfully and see how St. Basil, a beacon of orthodoxy in the early Church, explains the origin of the Church's teachings on sacramentals.

St. Justin Martyr, circa A.D. 150 — "And for this [the rite of baptism] we have learned from the Apostles this reason. Since at our birth we were born without our own knowledge or choice, by our parents coming together, and were brought up in bad habits and wicked training; in order that we may not remain the children of necessity and of ignorance, but may become the children of choice and knowledge, and may obtain in the water the remission of sins formerly committed, there is pronounced over him who chooses to be born again, and has repented of his sins, the name of God the Father and Lord of the universe; he who leads to the laver the person that is to be washed calling him by this name alone. For no one can utter the name of the ineffable God. . . . And this washing is called illumination, because they who learn these things are illuminated in their understandings. And in the name of Jesus Christ, who was crucified under Pontius Pilate, and in the name of the Holy Ghost, who through the prophets foretold all things about Jesus, he who is illuminated is washed" (*First Apology* 61).

Tertullian, circa A.D. 200 — "After this, when we have issued from the font, we are thoroughly anointed with a blessed unction, [a practice derived] from the old discipline, wherein on entering the priesthood, then were wont to be anointed with oil from a horn, ever since Aaron was anointed by Moses. Whence Aaron is called 'Christ,' from the 'chrism,' which is 'the unction'; which, when made spiritual, furnished an appropriate name to the Lord, because He was 'anointed' with the Spirit by God the Father; as written in the Acts: 'For truly they were gathered together in this city against Thy Holy Son whom Thou hast anointed.' Thus, too, in our case, the unction runs carnally [i.e., on the body], but profits spiritually; in the same way as the act of baptism itself too is carnal, in that we are plunged in water, but the effect spiritual, in that we are freed from sins" (*On Baptism* 7).

St. Basil the Great, A.D. 375 — "Of the beliefs and practices whether generally accepted or publicly enjoined which are preserved in the Church some we possess derived from written teaching; others we have received delivered to us 'in a mystery' by the tradition of the Apostles; and both of these in relation to true religion have the same force. And these no one will gainsay; no one, at all events, who is even moderately versed in the institutions of the Church. For were we to attempt to reject such customs as have no written authority, on the ground that the importance they possess is small [i.e., because they are not found in Scripture], we should unintentionally injure the Gospel in its very vitals; or, rather, should make our public definition a mere phrase and nothing more.

"For instance, to take the first and most general example, who is thence who has taught us in writing to sign with the sign of the cross those who have trusted in the name of our Lord Jesus Christ? What writing has taught us to turn to the East at the prayer? Which of the saints has left us in writing the words of the invocation at the displaying of the bread of the Eucharist and the cup of blessing? For we are not, as is well known, content with what the apostle or the Gospel has recorded, but both in preface and conclusion we add other words as being of great importance to the validity of the ministry, and *these we derive from unwritten teaching* [emphasis mine].

"Moreover we bless the water of baptism and the oil of the chrism, and besides this the catechumen who is being baptized. On what written authority do we do this? Is not our authority silent and mystical tradition? Nay, by what written word is the anointing of oil itself taught?

"And whence comes the custom of baptizing thrice? And as to the other customs of baptism, from what Scripture do we derive the renunciation of Satan and his angels? Does not this come from that unpublished and secret teaching which our fathers guarded in a silence out of the reach of curious meddling and inquisitive investigation? Well had they learnt the lesson that the awful [i.e., awesome] dignity of the mysteries is best preserved by silence. . . .

"In the same manner the Apostles and Fathers who laid down laws for the Church from the beginning thus guarded the awful dignity of the mysteries in secrecy and silence. . . . This is the reason for our tradition of unwritten precepts and practices, that the knowledge of our dogmas may not become neglected and contemned [i.e., scorned] by the multitude through familiarity. 'Dogma' and 'Kerygma' are two distinct things; the former is observed in silence; the latter is proclaimed to all the world. One form of this silence is the obscurity employed in Scripture, which makes the meaning of 'dogmas' difficult to be understood for the very advantage of the reader: Thus we all look to the East at our prayers, but few of us know that we are seeking our own old country, Paradise, which God planted in Eden in the East. We pray standing, on the first day of the week, but we do not all know the reason. On the day of the Resurrection we remind ourselves of the grace given to us by standing at prayer, not only because we rose with Christ, and are bound to 'seek those things which are above,' but because the day seems to us to be in some sense an image of the age which we expect [i.e., the day of our entrance into heavenly glory]. . . .

"[E]very time we fall upon our knees and rise from off them we shew by the very deed that by our sin we fell down to earth, and by the loving kindness of our Creator were called back to heaven. Time will fail me if I attempt to recount the unwritten mysteries of the Church" (*On the Holy Spirit* 27).

23. The Use of Incense and Candles in Liturgical Functions

Incense is a rich symbol of our prayers ascending to God. A sweet-smelling offering of praise and worship is the analogy that incense conveys to the senses. The liturgical use of incense in the Temple ceremonies was integral to Jewish worship for centuries (cf. Exodus 30:7-8; Leviticus 4:7; 1 Kings 9:25). In the Book of Revelation St. John describes his awesome vision of the heavenly liturgy in which he sees incense offered to the Lord, and he says that incense "mingled with the prayers of the holy ones" (cf. Revelation 8:3-4). The symbolism reminds us both of the prayers of the holy ones as well as the "fragrance of Christ" St. Paul speaks about poetically in 2 Corinthians 2:14-16.

The custom of using incense in the Liturgy arose from the deep association the early Christians saw between their Eucharistic Liturgy and that Old Testament sacred offering in the Temple that only imperfectly foreshadowed it: the "shewbread" that was offered by the high priest in the Holy of Holies inside the Temple (cf. Exodus 25:23-29, 26:31, 37:17-25; Hebrews 9:2-4). This special offering of bread by the priest prefigured and foreshadowed the perfect offering of Christ the High priest in the Eucharist. And just as the Old Testament offering took place at the "golden altar of incense" (cf. Exodus 30:1-10), the ancient Christian offering of the Eucharistic Sacrifice was also often accompanied by the use of incense as a way to show forth the sublime reality of Christ's presence in the Eucharistic elements being offered to the Father.

This powerful New Testament image of incense was deeply embedded in the mind of the early Church (cf. Luke 1:10; Revelation 8:3-4). Though some commentators assert that incense was not used liturgically in the earliest centuries of the Church, there is evidence that indicates that even in the first few centuries, incense was a part of the Eucharistic Liturgies in at least some places, especially in the East. Once the Catholic Church came out of hiding when Emperor Constantine relaxed and then eliminated the imperial bans on Christianity, we see the tradition of the liturgical use of incense gain momentum everywhere, especially during solemn Masses and other special ceremonies.

This was because Christians were reminded of biblical descriptions of incense, such as that in Psalm 141, which describes incense as billowing clouds of prayer ascending to God's throne in heaven. The tradition of using incense became for Christians, as it had been for the Jews in the Old Testament era, a powerful symbol for the prayers of the people and of their sacrifice, which in the case of the Christians is Christ himself in the Eucharist.

By the fourth century, especially in the Eastern churches, we begin to see a more widespread use of incense at the Liturgy, along with stylized priestly vestments (beyond the earlier use of a pallium for archbishops and the stole for presbyters and deacons) and ceremonial altar candles (in earlier days, candles were used but were there for light, not for ceremonial significance). This practice gained ground quickly in the West and by the Middle Ages we can see a very widespread tradition of using incense and candles at Mass — a tradition that has, happily, persisted until our present day.

The Divine Liturgy of James, circa A.D. 400 — "Prayer of the incense at the beginning: Sovereign Lord Jesus Christ, O Word of God, who didst freely offer Thyself a blameless sacrifice upon the cross to

God even the Father, the coal of double nature, that didst touch the lips of the prophet with the tongs, and didst take away his sins, touch also the hearts of us sinners, and purify us from every stain, and present us holy beside Thy holy altar, that we may offer Thee a sacrifice of praise: and accept from us, Thy unprofitable servants, this incense as an odor of a sweet smell, and make fragrant the evil odor of our soul and body, and purify us with the sanctifying power of Thy all-holy Spirit: for Thou alone art holy, who sanctifies, and art communicated to the faithful; and glory becomes Thee, with Thy eternal Father, and Thy all-holy, and good, and quickening Spirit, now and ever, and to all eternity. Amen" (*Divine Liturgy of St. James* 3).

The Divine Liturgy of St. James — "[The priest sings the prayer of the incense at the entrance of the congregation]: God, who didst accept the gifts of Abel, the sacrifice of Noah and of Abram, the incense of Aaron and of Zechariah, accept also from the hand of us sinners this incense for an odor of a sweet smell, and for remission of our sins, and those of all Thy people; for blessed art Thou, and glory becomes Thee, the Father, and the Son, and the Holy Spirit, now and ever" (*Divine Liturgy of St. James* 5).

Dionysius the Pseudo–Areopagite, circa A.D. 500 — "Wherefore that first institution of the sacred rites, judging it worthy of a supermundane copy of the Celestial Hierarchies, gave us our most holy Hierarchy, and described that spiritual Hierarchy in material terms and in various compositions of forms so that we might be led, each according to his capacity, from the most holy imagery to [unseen heavenly realities]. . . . For the mind can by no means be directed to the spiritual presentation and contemplation of the Celestial Hierarchies unless it use the material guidance suited to it, accounting those beauties which are seen to be images of the hidden beauty, *the sweet incense a symbol of spiritual dispensations*, and the earthly lights [i.e., candles] a figure of the immaterial enlightenment [i.e., the light of glory in heaven supplied by God Himself]" (*The Celestial Hierarchy* 3; emphasis mine).

24. Novenas and Special Prayers

The tradition of making novenas (from the Latin *novem*, meaning "nine") has a long history in Catholic spirituality. Today, though, some Protestants (and even, sadly, some poorly catechized Catholics) regard novenas as a superstition in the category of the "vain repetition" prayers the Lord condemned in Matthew 6:7.

The 2002 edition of *Our Sunday Visitor's Catholic Almanac* defines novena as "a term designating public or private devotional practices over a period of nine consecutive days; or, by extension, over a period of nine weeks, in which one day a week is set aside for the devotions."[86] Technically, a novena lasts nine days, but longer or shorter intervals of prayer can also be thought of as novenas. For example, Christ made a forty-day "novena" in the desert by fasting and praying in preparation for his public ministry. Indeed, the evidence in Scripture for making a novena is wide and deep.

In Acts 1:13-14 and Acts 2:1 we read that the Apostles, the Blessed Virgin Mary, and other holy women gathered in Jerusalem and spent the nine days between the Lord's Ascension and the day of Pentecost in intense prayer and contemplation. This first and greatest New Testament novena culminated on Pentecost with the descent of the Holy Spirit.

In Acts 9:9, Paul made a post-conversion "mini-novena" (three days) of intense prayer at the home of Ananias.

The Old Testament invests certain numbers (such as three, seven, twelve, and forty) with symbolic meaning. The "ninth hour" figures prominently in the New Testament. Jesus died at the ninth hour,[87] and the apostles frequently gathered to pray in the temple at the ninth hour.[88] St. Jerome wrote that "[t]he number nine in Holy Scripture is indicative of suffering and grief" (*Commentary on Ezekiel* 7:24).

In the Middle Ages the most common form of novena was the novena of preparation. It included the recitation of special prayers on each of the nine days before Christmas in honor of the nine months our Lord spent in the womb of the Blessed Virgin Mary. This practice flourished in Spain and France as early as the seventh century, but it was only in the seventeenth century that the pre-Christmas novena of preparation caught on in Italy (although novenas for deceased popes and cardinals had been celebrated there for centuries and, in Sicily, it was common for religious communities to observe novenas the nine days prior to the feast day of their founder).

But what about the charge that novenas, which are simply formula prayers repeated at nine intervals, are condemned by Jesus in Matthew 6:7?

The fact is that Jesus did *not* condemn formula prayers. This is demonstrated in the very next verse in Matthew 6, where the Lord gave us the best of all formula prayers, the Our Father. Christ's teaching in Matthew 6:7 is also not a condemnation of the repetition of prayers, per se. We know this because after teaching us *the* formula prayer — the Our Father — Jesus, in Luke 21:36, told us to "pray always." Paul echoed this need for continual prayer in 1 Thessalonians 5:17 and in 1 Timothy 2:8.

The Old Testament also corroborates the concept of repeating formula prayers. The Psalms were written for the express purpose of being sung or prayed repeatedly, week after week, in the synagogues. It's important to keep in mind that the Holy Spirit — God himself — inspired these repetitious prayers in order that they be used by his people. In other words, God himself intended that these prayers be repeated, just as he inspired the writers to set them down on paper. Examples of this kind of divinely inspired "repetitious prayer" are seen in passages such as Psalm 136 (where the refrain "for his mercy endures forever" repeats twenty-six times in a row!) and Daniel 3:52-90 (where the refrains "Blessed are you . . . praiseworthy and exalted forever" and "Praise and exalt him above all forever" are repeated many times).

Let's focus on the meaning of Jesus' condemnation of "vain repetition." It pivots on his use of the word "vain" — not, as is commonly thought by Protestants, on the word "repetition."

At the time of Christ, pagans went through a litany of titles when addressing their gods. They believed that if they didn't use the correct "title of the day" when invoking the god they were supplicating, the god would petulantly refuse to hear their prayers.

In order to solve this dilemma, the pagans resorted to "scattershot" litanies of great length designed to mention any conceivable title the god might desire to be called by that day. Completely aside from the biblical condemnation of praying to false gods (cf. Exodus 20:4-5), Jesus condemned the uselessness (vainness) of the pagan prayer hoopla, complete with its elaborate titles and endless repetitions, precisely because the gods weren't up there to hear it.

Pagan periods of special prayers bear nothing more than a passing resemblance to Catholic novenas. Those who condemn novenas as "pagan" should remember that by using the same logic, one could condemn fasting, hymn singing, meeting for worship on a particular day of the week, and even praying itself, simply because pagans also did all these things.[89]

Nonetheless, St. Augustine warned against the practice of novenas in the event they were observed either to mimic the pagans or for any superstitious qualities Christians might (wrongly) ascribe to them. Wise counsel indeed, but it seems clear that most early Christians, when praying special prayers for a fixed period of time, avoided any semblance of pagan superstition. In the mid-300s, we see the anonymous *Apostolic Constitutions*, as an example, refer to the practice of special prayers, such as novenas, being prayed for various intentions in the early Church (cf. 7:43). By the medieval era, the practice of novenas had become widespread throughout Christian Europe and elsewhere.

25. The Fixed Celebration of Christmas

The Catholic Church's decision to celebrate Christmas on December 25, and the resulting tradition of "Christmas,"[90] has drawn a lot of criticism from people who think this move was simply a sleight-of-hand move by the Church to absorb a pagan feast day into the Christian liturgical calendar. Not so.

In the first two centuries of the Church, Christmas was not a feast day. None of the lists of feast days compiled during that time include Christmas. However, by the year 200, the Christian desire to celebrate the birth of the Lord was coming into view. The tradition of celebrating the Nativity of the Lord was not fixed to a certain date. Some Christians, such as some in Egypt, observed the celebration in mid-May. Others commemorated the Lord's birth in March and April, doing their best to calculate the nine months he was in the womb of the Blessed Virgin Mary and, therefore, when he might have been born. Obviously, this was a wholly inexact effort, but it does show us that it was becoming increasingly important to the early Christians to observe with Masses, prayers, and hymns the memory of the Lord's birth.

By the mid-fourth century, we have clear evidence from the writings of the day that there was a formal observance of Christmas in Jerusalem, Bethlehem, and elsewhere in that region. And around the year 380, St. Gregory Nazianzen, bishop of Constantinople, declared the Nativity of the Lord to be a special feast day in the church there. All of these examples of Christians gradually adopting this feast day are marked by opposition from other Christians, including some notable Church Fathers. It seems clear that the issue of celebrating the birthday of the Lord was at variance, at least initially, with the universal Christian custom of observing the date of a Christian's baptism or, more commonly, his death — the day on which he was "reborn" into the eternal life in heaven. For some Christians, such as Origen, the celebration of one's natural birthday smacked of paganism and a carnal (i.e., non-spiritual) emphasis on the things of the world.[91]

But this suspicious view of celebrating the Nativity soon gave way to the rising Christian desire to celebrate the great event of the birth of the Lord. The vexing problem for this tradition, though, was that the Christians settled on the same date for their celebration of the Nativity as some pagans, especially Mithraists, observed for the celebration of the "sun god," *Sol Invictus* (Latin for "The Unconquerable Sun").

This tension between the Christian observance of this feast day for Christ's honor and the pagan observance of a false god caused a lot of friction. Early on, we see Christian writers going out of their way to distinguish between this laudable Christian practice and the coincidental usage of the same date by the pagans.

Around the year 250, **St. Cyprian of Carthage** declared: "Oh, how wonderfully [God's] Providence acted that on that day on which that sun [referring to the pagan notion of the 'sun god'] was born . . . that Christ should be born."

Similarly, **St. John Chrysostom** preached that "Our Lord, too, is born in the month of December . . . the eight before the calends of January [December 25]. . . , But they call it the 'Birthday of the Unconquered' [i.e., the 'sun god']. Who indeed is so unconquered as Our Lord . . . ? Or, if they say that it is the birthday of the Sun, He is the Sun of Justice [i.e., Jesus Christ]."[92] Similar statements about the celebration of Christ's birth on December 25 are found in the writings of St. Augustine (*Tractate 34 on the Gospel of John*), Tertullian (*Apology* 16), and Pope Leo the Great (Sermon 37, *On the Nativity of the Lord*).

The fact that the Church decided to adopt December 25 as the date for Christmas, the same date as the pagan celebration of *Sol Invictus*, should not trouble us. Here we see the triumph of Christ over paganism. The very fact that the Church's observance of the Nativity on December 25 supplanted (and eventually extinguished) the competing pagan custom shows the truth and power of Christianity. There never has been any sort of "pagan connection" between Christmas and pagan celebrations on December 25. Rather, this traditional feast day is an example of the power of Christian piety and love for Christ to overcome even the most entrenched pagan aberrations.

One final thought on this issue. In modern times, a similar controversy over the observance of the secular festival of "Halloween" has arisen. Many suspicious Protestants — and even some Catholics — look askance at the practice of children dressing up in costumes and roaming, door to door, in their neighborhoods knocking on doors and saying, "Trick or treat." The critics of Halloween fear that this is simply a pagan cultic practice that no Christian should be associated with. Fair enough. And without getting into the details of the issues surrounding the Halloween controversy, it's enough to point out that many Protestant churches, in an effort to keep their congregations away from the "trick or treat" observance of what they see as a pagan festival, will sponsor their own "Harvest Celebration" or some other similarly titled event that is held on the night of October 31. They do this to "Christianize" what they see as a pagan event, and their instincts are correct. This is precisely what the Catholic Church did over time in the early Church. Rather than simply tell the faithful to stay home on the particular days that pagans celebrated their false gods, the Church gradually began to hold her own celebrations on those days as a way to keep Christians away from paganism and to draw the pagans away from their futile rituals into the light and life of Jesus Christ and his Church.

26. Latin as the Official Language of the Western Church

The original "language of the Catholic Church" was Aramaic, followed closely by Hebrew. These were the languages spoken by Christ and the Apostles during the era of his public ministry in Palestine. The first

Mass (i.e., the Last Supper; cf. Matthew 26, Mark 14, Luke 22) was no doubt celebrated by Christ in Hebrew or Aramaic.

After the Day of Pentecost, the Apostles fanned out across the known world spreading the Faith and making converts. Because Greek was the primary language of the Mediterranean world, most of the Eucharistic Liturgies celebrated in the first two centuries would have been in Greek, for in the decades after Christ this language was commonly spoken by Jews and Gentiles alike in Asia Minor, Spain, Egypt, North Africa, Arabia, and Palestine. But in the latter part of the second century, Imperial Rome's native language of Latin had made great inroads and had, at least in the West, become the more commonly spoken tongue. We see evidence by the third century that the Eucharistic Liturgies were becoming increasingly common in Latin, certainly on the Italian peninsula.

Due to the influence of Greek upon Latin, there gradually emerged two distinct but closely related forms of Latin: *classical* (the more sophisticated and elegant Latin that was spoken by the elite class and written by Cicero and other Roman writers and orators) and vulgar (popularly meaning "crude" but in this case "common" — the less sophisticated Latin that was spoken by the common man). The Church became aware that it would be better to use the form of Latin that served the widest audience of Christians and potential converts, so the vulgate Latin became the accepted form of Church Latin (also called "ecclesiastical Latin"). As the Roman Liturgies were written down in the third and fourth centuries, we see the gradual emergence of Latin as the predominant language.

Major Church Fathers such as St. Jerome and St. Augustine propelled the use of Latin into the wider Western Church. So by the Middle Ages, Latin had become the *lingua franca* of the West, while Greek retained its ascendancy in the East. Even today, Latin is the official language of the Catholic Church, though we have in the last fifty years seen a dramatic tilt in the direction of English as the new universal tongue. We should never forget that the reason the Catholic Church eventually mandated that the Mass be celebrated in Latin (the same with Scripture in Latin, etc.) was precisely so that the greatest number of people everywhere would have unimpeded access to the sacraments and to the Scriptures. Some critics of the Church argue (wrongly) that the Church "imposed" Latin as a way to keep the common people "in the dark" about God's Word. But that's exactly the opposite of why it happened. The Church wanted then, as she does now, to make sure the message of Christ is accessible to all people.

27. The Origin of the Word 'Mass'

The Eucharistic Liturgy (i.e., in the Orthodox and Eastern Churches, the "Divine Liturgy") began to be known as the Mass by the end of the second century. This tradition gained ground quickly in the West as a result of the Latin phrase at the end of the Liturgy: *"Ite, Missa est,"* which means: "Go, you are [or 'it is'] sent." That concluding statement by the priest conveyed the missionary character of the participants in the Mass echoing the words of the Lord as he was about to ascend into heaven from the Mount of Olives. Here, Christ was officially sending the Church forth on its mission of bringing the Gospel to all the world: "Go [Latin: *ite*], therefore, and make disciples of all nations, baptizing them in the name of the Father, and of the Son, and of the holy Spirit, teaching them to observe all that I have commanded you. And behold, I am with you always, until the end of the age" (Matthew 28:19-20, NAB).

St. Ambrose of Milan, circa A.D. 380 — "The next day (it was a Sunday) after the lessons and the tract [i.e., the Scripture readings], having dismissed the catechumens, I explained the creed to some of the competents [people about to be baptized] in the baptistry of the basilica. There I was told suddenly that they [i.e., the Arians] had sent soldiers to the Portiana basilica. . . . But I remained at my place and began to say Mass [*missam facere coepi*]" (*Epistle* 1:20:4-5).

---

28. Mass on Sunday Instead of on the Sabbath

St. Justin Martyr wrote a letter to the Roman emperor around A.D. 155 in which he provides a glimpse into why the early Church had adopted the tradition of celebrating the Eucharistic Liturgy (i.e., the Mass, Divine Liturgy) on Sundays:

> "On the day we call the day of the sun,[93] all who dwell in the city or country gather in the same place. The memoirs [i.e., the readings from the Old and New Testaments] of the Apostles and the writings of the prophets are read, as much as time permits. When the reader has finished, he who presides over those gathered [i.e., the bishop or priest who then preaches a sermon on the theme of the readings] admonishes and challenges them to imitate these beautiful things.
>
> "Then we all rise together and offer prayers for ourselves . . . and for all others, wherever they may be, so that we may be found righteous by our

life and actions, and faithful to the commandments, so as to obtain eternal salvation. When the prayers are concluded we exchange the kiss [i.e., the sign of peace]. Then someone brings bread and a cup of water and wine mixed together to him who presides over the brethren. He takes them and offers praise and glory to the Father of the universe, through the name of the Son and of the Holy Spirit and for a considerable time he gives thanks [in Greek: *eucharistian*] that we have been judged worthy of these gifts. When he has concluded the prayers and thanksgivings, all present give voice to an acclamation by saying: 'Amen.' When he who presides has given thanks and the people have responded, those whom we call deacons give to those present the 'eucharisted' bread, wine and water and take them to those who are absent."

This wonderful passage shows us, among other things, that it was the very early custom for Christians to celebrate Mass on Sunday.

Similarly, we can also see this tradition in full swing in the *Didache*[94] (written around A.D. 100):

"But every Lord's Day, gather yourselves together, and break bread, and give thanksgiving after having confessed your transgressions, that your sacrifice may be pure. But let no one who is at odds with his fellow come together with you, until they be reconciled, that your sacrifice may not be profaned. For this is that which was spoken by the Lord: 'In every place and time offer to me a pure sacrifice; for I am a great King, says the Lord, and my name is wonderful among the nations'" (paragraph 14; the writer of the *Didache* is here quoting Malachi 1:11).

These statements from the early Church reflect the tradition that was already prevalent at the time of the Apostles (cf. Acts 20:7; 1 Corinthians 16:2). In fact, in the Book of Revelation, St. John the Apostle refers to Sunday as "The Lord's Day." It is pure conjecture, but still very possible, that when John spoke about being "caught up in the Spirit on the Lord's Day," he may very well have received this blessed vision from the Lord during or shortly after the "celebration of Mass" by Jesus. The mystical connection between the Mass and the Book of Revelation is profound![95]

The Catholic Church adopted this tradition of celebrating Mass on Sunday for two primary reasons. First, to honor and commemorate the Resurrection of the Lord on the first day of the week. Second, to draw a distinction between the Old Covenant observance of the day of rest on the Sabbath. The early Christians saw the benefit, both for themselves and those outside the Church, to show that the new Faith was distinct from the Jewish religion whence it sprang. By transferring observance of the Third Commandment — "Keep holy the Sabbath" (Exodus 20:8) — from the Jewish day of observance to Sunday, the day the Lord rose from the dead, the early Catholic Church was showing a definitive break with her Jewish roots. As St. Paul reminded the early Christians on this subject, "Let no one, then, pass judgment on you in matters of food and drink or with regard to a festival or new moon or sabbath" (Colossians 2:16; NAB). These (i.e., the Old Testament Jewish Sabbath) are shadows of things to come. The reality "belongs to Christ" (Colossians 2:16-17). The early Christians realized this truth keenly and wanted to live out that reality through their observance of Sunday as the day of rest the Lord commanded in Exodus 20.

The first day of the week, Sunday, as opposed to the Sabbath, Saturday, is often a point of contention with those, such as Seventh-Day Adventists, who claim Christians should still worship on the Sabbath. What can we say in response to that argument? First, let's point out that the commandment from God to "keep holy the Sabbath" is an eternal one that requires obedience from all Christians. The Catholic Church is clear that we cannot dispense with this (or any other) of the Ten Commandments.[96] Even so, some will still argue that Catholics are *not* following the Ten Commandments, indeed they are violating them, by transferring the observance of the Third Commandment from the Sabbath to the first day of the week. Usually, such complaints are couched in the form of a challenge that the Catholic Church changed an "eternal commandment" of God. Catholics should point out that if they are to follow their own logic, Seventh-Day Adventists themselves would be guilty of the same thing. This is because in Genesis 17:9-14, God commanded Abraham and his descendants:

> "As for you, you shall keep my covenant, you and your descendants after you throughout their generations. This is my covenant, which you shall keep, between me and you and your descendants after you: Every male among you shall be circumcised. You shall be circumcised in the flesh of your foreskins, and it shall be a sign of the covenant between me and you. He that is eight days old among you shall be circumcised; every male *throughout your generations*, whether born in your house, or bought with your money from any foreigner who is not of your offspring, both he that is born in your house and he that is bought with your money, shall be

circumcised. So shall my covenant be in your flesh an everlasting covenant. Any uncircumcised male who is not circumcised in the flesh of his foreskin shall be cut off from his people; he has broken my covenant" (Genesis 17:9-14, RSV; emphasis mine).

What makes this passage crucial for discussion with Seventh-Day Adventists and others who take potshots at the Catholic Church over the Third Command- ment is that they themselves are in direct violation of this very commandment to perform ritual circumci- sion for "all generations." Seventh-Day Adventists do not observe the Lord's commandment to perform cir- cumcision. Why not? Because they accept the Catho- lic Church's teaching that after the time of Christ, circumcision was done away with, as St. Paul explains in passages such as 1 Corinthians 7:19, Galatians 6:15, and Colossians 3:11.

But notice that it was a *man* (St. Paul), not God himself (Jesus Christ nowhere spoke about abolishing circumcision), who mentions that the Church began to observe that eternal commandment and covenant in a different way than it had originally been promul- gated by God to Abraham.[97] This is an important par- allel with the Sabbath/Sunday controversy. For if the early Church had the authority to modify the way in which the commandment of circumcision was car- ried out — which she did and still does (cf. Matthew 16:18, 18:18; Luke 10:16), as Seventh-Day Adventists are forced to admit, since they themselves don't prac- tice circumcision — then similarly, the Church had (and continues to have) the authority, given her by Christ her founder, to alter the way in which Chris- tians are to observe the Third Commandment to "keep holy the Lord's Day."

29. The Elevation of the Host at Mass

This practice (tradition) of the priest elevating the sacred host began in Paris, France, in the year 1210 by direction of the archbishop there. He was concerned that there could be confusion among the faithful about when the Eucharistic elements were transubstantiated from bread and wine into the Body and Blood as well as the soul and divinity of the Lord. The potential for confusion stemmed from the fact that, prior to this modification, the priest, who was facing toward the altar and away from the congregation, held the sacred host in front of him, which meant the congregation behind him were unable to see the host during the consecration. The archbishop wanted to ensure that the faithful adored Christ in the Eucharist once the consecration had taken place, and not before (which would have constituted the material sin of idolatry, for worshipping bread). The tradition of elevating the host (and chalice) at the consecration quickly became popular and spread rapidly to the Western Church as a whole.

30. The Sign of the Cross

This is one of the most ancient customs in the Catholic Church. From time immemorial, Christians have observed the pious custom of tracing the sign of the cross on their foreheads. The more common version of this practice, especially among Catholics and Orthodox, is the making of a large outline of the cross by hand, starting at the forehead, then to the center of the chest, then to the left shoulder, and then to the right shoulder. This tradition of blessing oneself and others with the sign of the cross arose very early in the Church and corresponds with the biblical passage where the Lord commanded his the Apostles to go forth into the world:

> "Go therefore and make disciples of all nations, baptizing them *in the name of the Father and of the Son and of the Holy Spirit*, teaching them to observe all that I have commanded you; and lo, I am with you always, to the close of the age"[98] (Matthew 28:19-20, RSV; emphasis mine).

This action of tracing the sign of the cross has roots deep within the Bible itself. Passages such as Ezekiel 9:4, Exodus 13:9, 16, and Revelation 7:3, 9:4, 14:1 remind us that the tracing of a "sign" or "seal" on the forehead was one way of showing that the person was set apart by God for special protection or blessings. This gesture also is vividly reminiscent of the Lord's command to Moses that the doorpost and lintels of each family's home should be marked with the blood of the slain Passover lamb as a sign of God's protection for that household. Similarly, when Catholics make the sign of the cross, they are invoking the grace and protection of the Lamb of God, the one who alone can protect and deliver us from eternal death. They are symbolically anointing the doorposts and lintels of their own bodies — the temple of the Holy Spirit — with the saving blood of Christ, as they repeat in faith the words of the Lord, "baptizing them in the name of the Father, and of the Son, and of the Holy Spirit." This grace-filled gesture is both a reminder of one's new birth in Christ through baptism (cf. Acts 2:37-39, 22:16; Colossians 2:11-12; Titus 3:4-7; 1 Hebrews 10:22; 1 Peter 3:21) as well as a reminder that

Christ alone, through his death and Resurrection, is the Lamb of God who saves us.

From what we can tell, making the sign of the cross was already a widely practiced Christian tradition as early as the second century. The *Catholic Encyclopedia* explains:

> "Of all the above methods of venerating this life-giving symbol [i.e., of the cross] and adopting it as an emblem, the marking of a little cross seems to be the most ancient. We have positive evidence in the early Fathers that such a practice was familiar to Christians in the second century. 'In all our travels and movements,' says **Tertullian** (*De Corona* iii), 'in all our coming in and going out, in putting on our shoes, at the bath, at the table, in lighting our candles, in lying down, in sitting down, whatever employment occupieth us, we mark our foreheads with the sign of the cross.'
>
> "On the other hand this must soon have passed into a gesture of benediction [i.e., blessing], as many quotations from the Fathers in the fourth century would show. Thus **St. Cyril of Jerusalem** in his *Catechetical Lectures* (13:36) remarks, 'Let us then not be ashamed to confess the Crucified. Be the cross our seal, made with boldness by our fingers on our brow and in every thing; over the bread we eat and the cups we drink, in our comings and in goings; before our sleep, when we lie down and when we awake; when we are traveling, and when we are at rest.'[99]

At Mass, when the Gospel is about to be read, the priest says, "A reading from the Holy Gospel, according to St. Luke" (or Mark, or Matthew, or John). The faithful respond with a heartfelt, "Glory to you, O

Lord Jesus Christ!" and trace a small sign of the cross with their thumb on their foreheads, on their lips, and over their hearts. This, gesture is also an ancient Christian custom, and is mentioned by St. Jerome (A.D. 340-420) in various places in his writings.

This universal ancient Christian tradition is not in itself doctrinal (remember, it's a "small-t" tradition); rather, it is a simple sacred gesture that is radically imbued with doctrinal truths, such as the Incarnation, the Atonement, grace and gratuitous salvation, the Trinity, etc. It is truly beautiful to see such deep and central doctrines of our Catholic Faith so succinctly summed up in such a modest gesture. Whenever we observe this tradition of making the sign of the cross, we are giving a flesh-and-blood testimony to the truth of what St. Paul said: "[W]e preach Christ *crucified*, a stumbling block to Jews and folly to Gentiles" (1 Corinthians 1:23, RSV; emphasis mine).

He goes on to say: "When I came to you, brothers, proclaiming the mystery of God, I did not come with sublimity of words or of wisdom. *For I resolved to know nothing while I was with you, except Jesus Christ, and him crucified*" (1 Corinthians 2:1-2, NAB; emphasis mine).

V. MORAL ISSUES

31. Contraception

The Catholic Church has always condemned artificial birth control — contraception — as being gravely sinful. When Pope Paul VI reiterated the Church's teaching on the subject of contraception, he wasn't saying anything new. Rather, he was simply restating what the Church had always held and taught, even from the earliest years of Christianity. Here are some representative examples of the early Church Fathers and other authoritative sources who act as monuments of this Tradition:

In A.D. 195, Clement of Alexandria wrote, "Because of its divine institution for the propagation of man, the seed is not to be vainly ejaculated, nor is it to be damaged, nor is it to be wasted" (*The Instructor of Children* 2:10:91:2).

St. Hippolytus of Rome, A.D. 255 — "[O]n account of their prominent ancestry and great property, the so-called faithful want no children from slaves or lowborn commoners, [so] they use drugs of sterility or bind themselves tightly in order to expel a fetus which has already been engendered" (*Refutation of All Heresies* 9:12).

Lactantius, A.D. 307 — "[Some people] complain of the scantiness of their means, and allege that they have not enough for bringing up more children, as though, in truth, their means were in [their] power . . . or God did not daily make the rich poor and the poor rich. Wherefore, if any one on any account of poverty shall be unable to bring up children, it is better to abstain from relations with his wife" (*Divine Institutes* 6:20).

The First Council of Nicaea, A.D. 325 — "If anyone in sound health has castrated himself, it behooves that such a one, if enrolled among the clergy, should cease [from his ministry], and that from hence-forth no such person should be promoted. But, as it is evident that this is said of those who willfully do the thing and presume to castrate themselves, so if any have been made eunuchs by barbarians, or by their masters, and should otherwise be found worthy, such men this canon admits to the clergy" (canon 1).

St. Augustine of Hippo, A.D. **419** — "I am sup-posing, then, although you are not lying [with your wife] for the sake of procreating offspring, you are not for the sake of lust obstructing their procreation by an evil prayer or an evil deed. Those who do this, al-though they are called husband and wife, are not; nor do they retain any reality of marriage, but with a re-spectable name cover a shame. Sometimes this lustful cruelty, or cruel lust, comes to this, that they even procure poisons of sterility. . . . Assuredly if both hus-band and wife are like this, they are not married, and if they were like this from the beginning, they come together not joined in matrimony but in seduction" (*Marriage and Concupiscence* 1:15:17).

32. Abortion

The Catholic Church has always condemned abor-tion — the intentional killing of an unborn child — as being gravely sinful. Here are some representative examples of the early Church Fathers and other au-thoritative sources who act as monuments of this Tradition:

The *Didache*,[100] **circa** A.D. **70–80** — "The sec-ond commandment of the teaching: You shall not mur-der. You shall not commit adultery. You shall not se-duce boys. You shall not commit fornication. You shall not steal. You shall not practice magic. You shall not use potions. You shall not procure [an] abortion, nor destroy a newborn child" (2:1).

The *Epistle of Barnabas,* A.D. **74** — "The way of light, then, is as follows. If any one desires to travel to the appointed place, he must be zealous in his works. The knowledge, therefore, which is given to us for the purpose of walking in this way, is the following. . . . Thou shalt not slay the child by procuring abortion; nor, again, shalt thou destroy it after it is born" (section 19).

Athenagoras, A.D. **177** — "What man of sound mind, therefore, will affirm, while such is our character, that we are murderers? . . . when we say that those women who use drugs to bring on abortion commit murder, and will have to give an account to God for the abortion, on what principle should we commit murder? For it does not belong to the same person to regard the very fetus in the womb as a created being, and therefore an object of God's care, and when it has passed into life, to kill it; and not to expose an infant, because those who expose them are chargeable with child-murder, and on the other hand, when it has been reared to destroy it" (*A Plea for the Christians* 35).

Tertullian, A.D. **197** — "In our case, a murder being once for all forbidden, we may not destroy even the fetus in the womb, while as yet the human being derives blood from the other parts of the body for its sustenance. To hinder a birth is merely a speedier man-killing; nor does it matter whether you take away a life that is born, or destroy one that is coming to birth. That is a man which is going to be one; you have the fruit already in its seed" (*Apology*[101] 9:8).

Tertullian, A.D. **210** — "Among surgeons' tools there is a certain instrument, which is formed with a nicely-adjusted flexible frame for opening the uterus first of all and keeping it open; it is further furnished with an annular blade, by means of which the limbs [of the child] within the womb are dissected with anxious but unfaltering care; its last appendage being a blunted or covered hook, wherewith the entire fetus is extracted by a violent delivery. There is also a copper needle or spike, by which the actual death is managed in this furtive robbery of life. They give it, from its infanticide function, the name of *embruosphaktes*, [which means] "the slayer of the infant," which of course was alive [in the womb] . . ." (*On the Soul* 25).

Tertullian — "[They] all knew well enough that a living being had been conceived, and pitied this most luckless infant state, which had first to be put to death, to escape being tortured alive. . . . Now we allow that life begins with conception because we contend that the soul also begins from conception, life taking its commencement at the same moment and place that the soul does" (*On the Soul* 27).

Minucius Felix, A.D. 226 — "There are some women who, by drinking medical preparations, extinguish the source of the future man in their very bowels and thus commit a parricide before they bring forth. And these things assuredly come down from the teaching of your gods [i.e., the false gods of paganism]. . . . To us [Christians] it is not lawful either to see or hear of homicide" (*Octavius* 30).

St. Hippolytus, A.D. 228 — "Women who were reputed to be believers began to take drugs to render themselves sterile, and to bind themselves tightly so as to expel what was being conceived, since they would not, on account of relatives and excess wealth, want to have a child by a slave or by any insignificant person. See, then, into what great impiety that lawless one has proceeded, by teaching adultery and murder at the same time!" (*Refutation of All Heresies* 9:7).

Lactantius, A.D. 307 — "When God forbids us to kill, he not only prohibits us from open violence, which is not even allowed by the public laws, but he warns us against the commission of those things which are esteemed lawful among men. Therefore, let no one imagine that even this is allowed, to strangle newly-born children, which is the greatest impiety; for God breathes into their souls for life, and not for death. But men, that there may be no crime with which they may not pollute their hands, deprive [unborn] souls as yet innocent and simple of the light which they themselves have not given.

"Can anyone, indeed, expect that they would abstain from the blood of others who do not abstain even from their own? But these are, without any controversy, wicked and unjust" (*Divine Institutes* 6:20).

The Synod of Ankara, A.D. 314 — "Concerning women who commit fornication, and destroy that which they have conceived, or who are employed in making drugs for abortion, a former decree excluded them until the hour of death, and to this some have assented. Nevertheless, being desirous to use somewhat greater lenity [i.e., gentleness or leniency], we have ordained that they fulfill ten years [of penance], according to the prescribed degrees" (canon 21).

St. Basil the Great, A.D. 374 — "Let her that procures abortion undergo ten years' penance, whether the embryo were perfectly formed, or not. . . . He that kills another with a sword, or hurls an axe at his own wife and kills her, is guilty of willful murder; not he who throws a stone at a dog, and unintentionally kills a man, or who corrects one with a rod, or scourge, in order to reform him, or who kills a man in his own defense, when he only designed to hurt him. But the man, or woman, is a murderer that gives a *philtrum* [i.e., a potion or drug], if the man that takes it die upon it; so are they who take medicines to procure abortion; and so are they who kill on the highway, and *rapparees* [i.e., plunderers or vagabonds]" (*First Canonical Letter* 2:8).

St. John Chrysostom, A.D. 391 — "Wherefore I beseech you, flee fornication. . . . Why sow where the ground makes it its care to destroy the fruit? — where there are many efforts at abortion? — where there is murder before the birth? For even the harlot you do not let continue a mere harlot, but make her a murderess also. You see how drunkenness leads to prostitution, prostitution to adultery, adultery to murder; or rather to a something even worse than murder. For I have no name to give it, since it does not take off the thing born, but prevents its being born. Why then do thou abuse the gift of God, and fight with His laws, and follow after what is a curse as if a blessing, and make the chamber of procreation a chamber for murder, and arm the woman that was given for childbearing unto slaughter? For with a view to drawing more money by being agreeable and an object of longing to her lovers, even this she is not backward to do, so heaping upon thy head a great pile of fire. For even if the daring deed be hers, yet the causing of it is thine" (*Homilies on Romans* 24).

St. Jerome, A.D. 396 — "I cannot bring myself to speak of the many virgins who daily fall and are lost to the bosom of the Church, their mother. . . . Some go so far as to take potions, that they may insure barrenness, and thus murder human beings almost before their conception. Some, when they find themselves with child through their sin, use drugs to procure abortion, and when, as often happens, they die with their offspring, they enter the lower world laden with the guilt not only of adultery against Christ but also of suicide and child murder" (*Epistle* 22:13).

The Apostolic Constitutions, A.D. 400 — "Thou shalt not use magic. Thou shalt not use witchcraft; for He says, 'You shall not suffer a witch to live.'[102] Thou shall not slay thy child by causing abortion, nor kill that which is begotten; for 'everything that is shaped, and has received a soul from God, if it be slain, shall be avenged, as being unjustly destroyed'" (*Apostolic Constitutions* 7:3).

---

33. Numbering of the Ten Commandments

This is a vexing problem for many people. Protestants, Mormons, and Jehovah's Witnesses attack the Catholic Church's teaching on sacred images by appealing to scriptural passages that condemn idolatry, the most common verses being those in Exodus 20. Before we consider why the Catholic numbering of the commandments is different from the way Protestants typically number them, let's first simply look at how they are given in Scripture:

> "And God spoke all these words, saying,
> "'I am the LORD your God, who brought you out of the land of Egypt, out of the house of bondage.
> "'You shall have no other gods before me.
> "'You shall not make for yourself a graven image, or any likeness of anything that is in heaven above, or that is in the earth beneath, or that is in the water under the earth; you shall not bow down to them or serve them; for I the LORD your God am a jealous God, visiting the iniquity of the fathers upon the children to the third and the fourth

generation of those who hate me, but showing steadfast love to thousands of those who love me and keep my commandments.

" 'You shall not take the name of the LORD your God in vain; for the LORD will not hold him guiltless who takes his name in vain.

" 'Remember the Sabbath day, to keep it holy. Six days you shall labor, and do all your work; but the seventh day is a sabbath to the LORD your God; in it you shall not do any work, you, or your son, or your daughter, your manservant, or your maid-servant, or your cattle, or the sojourner who is within your gates; for in six days the LORD made heaven and earth, the sea, and all that is in them, and rested the seventh day; therefore the LORD blessed the sabbath day and hallowed it.

" 'Honor your father and your mother, that your days may be long in the land which the LORD your God gives you.

" 'You shall not kill.

" 'You shall not commit adultery.

" 'You shall not steal.

" 'You shall not bear false witness against your neighbor.

" 'You shall not covet your neighbor's house; you shall not covet your neighbor's wife, or his manservant, or his maidservant, or his ox, or his ass, or anything that is your neighbor's' " (Exodus 20:1-17, RSV; cf. Deuteronomy 5).

The Catholic Numbering of the Commandments

For the sake of easy memorization, the Church historically has condensed or "distilled" the passage above into the Ten Commandments[103] we have learned since childhood:

I. Thou shalt have no strange gods before me.
II. Thou shalt not take the name of the Lord thy God in vain.
III. Keep holy the Sabbath.
IV. Honor your father and your mother.
V. Thou shalt not kill.
VI. Thou shalt not commit adultery.
VII. Thou shalt not steal.
VIII. Thou shalt not bear false witness.
IX. Thou shalt not covet thy neighbor's wife.
X. Thou shalt not covet thy neighbor's goods.

The Protestant Numbering of the Commandments
I. Thou shalt have no strange gods before me.
II. Thou shalt not carve graven images.
III. Thou shalt not take the name of the Lord thy God in vain.
IV. Keep holy the Sabbath.
V. Honor your father and your mother.
VI. Thou shalt not kill.
VII. Thou shalt not commit adultery.
VIII. Thou shalt not steal.
IX. Thou shalt not bear false witness.
X. Thou shalt not covet thy neighbor's wife, and thou shalt not covet thy neighbor's goods.

As we can see, Catholics combine two prohibitions of the Lord into one commandment — thou shalt not have strange gods before me (i.e., idolatry) and thou shalt not carve graven images nor bow down to and worship them (i.e., idolatry) — while Protestants *separate* those statements into two distinct commandments, and they combine into a single commandment the two very different sins of coveting your neighbor's wife and coveting his goods.

The *Catholic Encyclopedia* explains how this tradition arose and why, at the time of the Protestant Reformation, there was a deviation from the established Catholic practice of numbering the commandments:

"There is no numerical division of the Commandments in the Books of Moses (i.e., in the Hebrew text), but the injunctions are distinctly tenfold, and are found almost identical in both sources. The order, too, is the same except for the final prohibitions pronounced against concupiscence, that of Deuteronomy being adopted in preference to Exodus. A confusion, however, exists in the numbering, which is due to a difference of opinion concerning the initial precept on Divine worship.

"The system of numeration found in Catholic Bibles is based on the Hebrew text, was made by St. Augustine (fifth century) in his book of *Questions of Exodus* (*Quæstionum in Heptateuchum libri* VII, book II, question lxxi), and was adopted by the Council of Trent. It is followed also by the German Lutherans, except those of the school of Bucer. This arrangement makes the First Commandment relate to false worship and to the worship of false gods as to a single subject and a single class of sins to be guarded against — the reference to idols being regarded as mere application of the precept to adore but one God and the prohibition as directed against the particular offense of idolatry alone.

"According to this manner of reckoning, the injunction forbidding the use of the Lord's Name in vain comes second in order; and the decimal number is safeguarded by making a division of the final precept on concupiscence — the Ninth pointing to sins of the flesh and the Tenth to desires for unlawful possession of goods. Another division has been adopted by the English and Helvetian (i.e., Swiss) Protestant churches on the authority of Philo Judaeus, Josephus Origen, and others, whereby two Commandments are made to cover the matter of worship, and thus the numbering of the rest is advanced one higher; and the Tenth embraces both the Ninth and Tenth of the Catholic division. It seems, however, as logical to separate at the end as to group at the beginning, for while one single object is aimed at under worship, two specifically different sins are forbidden under covetousness; if adultery and theft belong to two distinct species of moral wrong, the same must be said of the desire to commit these evils."[104]

Protestants argue that Catholics are "hiding" part of the first commandment, the part about carving graven images, because we want to preserve our tradition of images even if it means going against the Ten Commandments. Nothing could be further from the truth. Here's the problem:

As it was alluded to above, the prohibitions in Exodus 20 against (1) worshipping false gods and (2) carving idols for the sake of worshipping them deal with the exact same sin: idolatry. The issue of idol worship happened to be a particularly common form of this sin, and God makes it clear that carving statues or fashioning images for the sake of worshipping them is evil. The Catholic Church rightly condenses both into the single commandment: don't worship false gods.

Also, the two prohibitions — don't covet your neighbor's goods and don't covet your neighbor's wife — are two very different kinds of sins (keep in mind the prohibitions against adultery and theft are universally seen by Catholics, Protestants, Jews, and others as distinct, separate kinds of sins). So when Protestants combine these two sins into a single commandment: thou shalt not covet your neighbor's goods or your neighbor's wife, they are making a mistake. It's wrong because it treats the sin of lust (adultery in one's heart) as if it were covetousness of an object (theft in one's heart). To put it a different way, it's one thing to covet your neighbor's lawnmower, but that kind of sin is totally different from coveting (lusting after) his wife (or her husband, in the case of women). Husbands and wives are people, not property, so it's clear that the offenses God warns against here are different.

As we have already seen in an earlier section of this book (as well as in my book *Where Is That in the Bible?*), the Catholic Church's teaching on the correct use of statues and images is totally consistent with what God commanded. The Catholic Church forbids the worship of graven images, just as it condemns the worship of any other false god. But the Church also recognizes that there is a correct use of statues and images in a religious context. God made that clear when just five chapters after his prohibition in Exodus 20 against carving graven images for the purpose of idolatry, he commands Moses to carve graven images of angels that would sit atop the Ark of the Covenant (cf. Exodus 25).

Clearly, God was not being schizophrenic. He didn't "forget" what he had said in Exodus 20. Rather, he was pointing out that there is a proper role for sacred images for believers, so long as they always avoid the abuse of that good thing through the sin of idolatry. This fact is true of so many Catholic Traditions and traditions that are rejected by non-Catholics, and we should always keep it in mind. If one simply plucks Bible passages out of context or without regard to related passages that shed light on a given subject, he runs the risk of veering off headlong into a distorted, erroneous understanding of the Bible. Without recognizing and embracing the unwritten Traditions that help the Church in every age correctly understand the message of the Gospel that comes down to us also in Scripture, he will be like the unfortunate people St. Peter warned about in 2 Peter 3:15-16.

There are many examples that could be given of Catholic Traditions and traditions that appear completely unbiblical, even *anti-biblical*, to Protestants, Mormons, and other non-Catholics simply because those people focus their arguments against Catholicism on one or two Bible verses, and they exclude or forget about related verses that would show that their argument is incorrect. As we saw with the Catholic and Orthodox tradition of calling priests "father," many will reject this traditional appellation because they are fixated on the Lord's words in Matthew 23:9 ("call no man father"), but they ignore passages such as Acts 7:2 (where St. Stephen, under the inspiration of the Holy Spirit, addresses the Jewish leaders as "my fathers") and 1 Corinthians 4:15 (where St. Paul reminds us, "I became your father in Christ Jesus through the gospel").

The Catholic tradition of calling priests "father," just one of many similar examples we could list, can be recognized for what it is — a holy and wholesome practice that honors God — only when the one objecting to that Tradition on the basis of a single passage is willing to consider the fact that there are other passages that put it into perspective. It's our mission as apostles for Christ to help people see the broader body of evidence that demonstrates the validity of Catholic Tradition and traditions.

A FINAL THOUGHT
ON TRADITION

Vatican II's document on Divine revelation, *Dei Verbum* (Latin for "the Word of God") summarized the essential unity of Scripture, Tradition, and the magisterium:

"It is clear, therefore, that sacred tradition, Sacred Scripture and the teaching authority of the Church [i.e., the magisterium], in accord with God's most wise design, are so linked and joined together that one cannot stand without the others, and that all together and each in its own way under the action of the one Holy Spirit contribute effectively to the salvation of souls" (DV 10).

This wise arrangement is Christ's doing, not man's. And it should be marvelous in our eyes. But, obviously, there are many non-Catholics for whom the word "marvelous" would not leap to mind when they consider Catholic Tradition.

Most people who reject Catholic Tradition do not do so out of malice or insincerity, and certainly not because they are stupid or slow-witted. No. Almost always, these people are sincere, they love God, and they want to obey his teachings. Their rejection of Tradition stems not from malice, but from their not having had an opportunity to hear the whole story about Tradition and see all the evidence that demonstrates that Catholic Tradition, as well as its customs and disciplines, are not "rabbits being pulled out of a hat" by unscrupulous priests bent on subverting God's Word. They have never had the doctrine of Tradition — what it is and what it isn't — explained to them in a way that makes sense. Many, as we saw earlier, think of Catholic Tradition as a two-thousand-year old game of "Telephone," a game in which the truths of the Faith have become so garbled and so intermixed with erroneous man-made notions that they bear little resemblance to what they imagine the "pure wheat" of the primitive Gospel must have contained. It's an understandable though completely incorrect assumption.

After all, we have Jesus Christ's word on it that he would protect his Church from teaching error: "He who listens to you, listens to me, and he who rejects you, rejects me" (cf. Luke 10:16); "Whatever you bind on earth will be bound in heaven, and whatever you loose on earth will be loosed in heaven" (cf. Matthew 16:18-19; 18:18).

He promised to be with His Church "until the end of the world" (cf. Matthew 28:20).

He promised he would send the Holy Spirit to the Church to "be with you always," to "teach you everything," and to guide the Church "into all truth" (cf. John 14:16, 25; 16:13). These passages and many others that could be adduced here imply the infallibility of the Church Christ established.

There is simply no way that he, as God, could deceive us by making false promises that when his Church teaches, it is he who teaches through the Church, or that the Holy Spirit will teach the Church all things and guide it into all truth. Christ's many promises on this issue point us unequivocally to the fact that he must have graced the Church with the charism of infallibility, a grace that prevents the Church from formally teaching error. If he had not done so, then the Church — *his* Church — would have been left completely vulnerable to the vagaries of erroneous human opinions and mistaken understandings of Scripture and the oral apostolic Traditions. But that did not happen; it cannot happen. As Christ promised, "I will not leave you orphans" (John 14:18, NAB).

These promises entail precisely the fact that the Tradition of Christ's Church, which is nothing less than the Church's lived interpretation of his teachings and those of the apostles, could not be compromised; it could not be contaminated by human error, and it would always and everywhere be faithfully and accurately handed on to each generation of Christians.

Christ's promises about the doctrinal integrity of his Church should gladden our hearts and encourage us to be better apostles, going out to the world with the message that the full Gospel of Jesus Christ, complete with all its written and unwritten Traditions, is found in its fullness only in the Catholic Church. It's a message that many non-Catholics may balk at, responding, "This is a hard saying; who can listen to it?"

The truth about Sacred Tradition is hard for some to accept, yes, but it is true nonetheless. And it's our duty as Catholics to do our best, aided by prayer, Scripture, and an appeal to the facts of Church history, to show our non-Catholic friends that Sacred Tradition is simply the ongoing lived interpretation of God's Word as it came to us in the deposit of faith from the lips of Christ and the preaching and writing of the Apostles, who taught with his own authority (cf. Luke 10:16). We should never forget the words of St. Paul on this subject:

> "So then, brethren, stand firm and hold to the traditions which you were taught by us, either by word of mouth or by letter" (2 Thessalonians 2:15, RSV).

In response to that exhortation, every Catholic can and should say with humble confidence, "By God's grace, for the last two thousand years, we have stood firm and held fast to the written and unwritten Traditions that were taught to us, we hold fast to them now, and we always will."

RECOMMENDED READING

An Essay on the Development of Christian Doctrine, the Venerable Cardinal John Henry Newman, University of Notre Dame Press, 1989 ed.

Any Friend of God's Is a Friend of Mine: A Biblical and Historical Explanation of the Catholic Doctrine of the Communion of Saints, Patrick Madrid, Basilica Press, 1996.

Tradition and Traditions, Cardinal Yves M. J. Congar, O.P., Burns and Oates, Ltd., 1966.

Theology of the Icon, Leonid Ouspensky, St. Vladimir's Seminar Press, 1978.

Where Is That in the Bible?, Patrick Madrid, Our Sunday Visitor Publishing, 2001.

The Faith of the Early Fathers, William Jurgens, ed., three volumes, The Liturgical Press, 1979.

Pope Fiction: Answers to 30 Myths and Misconceptions About the Papacy, Patrick Madrid, Basilica Press, 2000.

One, Holy, Catholic, and Apostolic, Kenneth Whitehead, Ignatius Press, 2000.

The Fathers of the Church, Mike Aquilina, Our Sunday Visitor Publishing, 2000.

The Mass of the Early Christians, Mike Aquilina, Our Sunday Visitor Publishing, 2001.

The Shepherd and the Rock: Origins, Development, and Mission of the Papacy, J. Michael Miller, C.S.B., Our Sunday Visitor Publishing, 1999.

Encyclopedia of Catholic Doctrine, Russell Shaw, ed., Our Sunday Visitor Publishing, 2001.

The Hidden Manna, James T. O'Connor, Ignatius Press, 1986.

Fundamentals of Catholic Dogma, Ludwig Ott, TAN Books, 1966 ed.

A History of Christendom, Warren Carroll, four volumes, Christendom College Press, 1985-2000.

The Christian Faith in the Doctrinal Documents of the Catholic Church, J. Neuner, S.J., and J. Dupuis, S.J., eds., Alba House, 1981.

Mary: A History of Doctrine and Devotion, Hilda Graef, Sheed & Ward, London, 1963.

Mary Through the Centuries: Her Place in the History of Culture, Jaroslav Pelikan, Yale University Press, 1998.

The Emergence of Catholic Tradition: A History of the Development of Doctrine, Jaroslav Pelikan, The University of Chicago Press, 1975.

Surprised by Truth 2, Patrick Madrid, Sophia Institute Press, 2000.

Search and Rescue: How to Bring Your Family and Friends Into — or Back Into — the Catholic Church, Patrick Madrid, Sophia Institute Press, 2001.

The Vindication of Tradition, Jaroslav Pelikan, Yale University Press, 1984.

Mary and the Fathers of the Church: The Blessed Virgin Mary in Patristic Thought, Luigi S. M. Gambero, Ignatius Press, 1999.

A History of Theology, Yves M. J. Congar, O.P., Doubleday and Co., 1968.

Envoy Magazine, edited by Patrick Madrid, contains hundreds of articles on doctrine and apologetics, www.envoymagazine.com.

The Catholic Answer, edited by Father Peter M. J. Stravinskas, a popular apologetics periodical published by Our Sunday Visitor Publishing (tcanswer@osv.com; 800-348-2440).

SOURCES

The following sources for the patristic quotations in this book are gratefully acknowledged:

William Jurgens, *The Faith of the Early Fathers* (Collegeville:The Liturgical Press, 1970), three volumes.

J. B. Lightfoot, J. R. Harmer (Michael W. Holmes, editor), *The Apostolic Fathers* (Grand Rapids, Mich.: Baker Book House Co., 2nd ed., 1989).

Philip Schaff, Henry Wace, editors, *The Early Church Fathers: Ante-Nicene, Nicene, and Post-Nicene Fathers* (Grand Rapids, Mich.: Eerdmans Publishing Co., 1979 ed.), 38 volumes.

Johannes Quasten, Joseph Plumpe, editors, *Ancient Christian Writers* (Westminster, Md.: The Newman Press, 1955 ed.), multi-volume.

The New Advent Supersite online Patristics Collection: www.newadvent.org/fathers.

The Christian Classics Ethereal Library: www.ccel.org/fathers/2/.

The St. Pachomius Orthodox Library, www.ocf.org/OrthodoxPage/reading/St.Pachomius/.

The Order of St. Benedict, *Lectio Divina*, www.osb.org/lectio/.

For further study, I also recommend the wonderful *Patrologia Latinae* database online patristics collection (the digital archives of Jacques-Paul Migne's magisterial collection, *Patrologia Latina*): http://pld.chadwyck.com.

ENDNOTES

1. Compare this passage to St. Paul's exhortation about Tradition in 2 Thessalonians 2:15.

2. St. Paul's exhortation to Timothy, "O Timothy, *guard what has been entrusted to you*" (1 Timothy 6:20, RSV; emphasis mine), is a direct allusion to the "deposit of faith." The magisterium of the Church, of which St. Timothy, as a bishop, was a member, has been charged by Christ with the mission of carefully safeguarding, authentically teaching, and faithfully transmitting the oral and written Traditions contained in the deposit of faith to each generation (cf. CCC 85-87).

3. When translating the Latin Vulgate from the original Greek and Hebrew, master Scripture scholar St. Jerome (A.D. 340-420) rendered the underlying Greek verb *paradidomi* into Latin as *traditae*, from the Latin verb *tradere*, which means to "to hand on" or, more literally, "to tradition" something to someone. There is no verb form of *tradere* ("to tradition") in English, so the phrase "handed on" is often used in translation, though that lacks the lexical force of the original Greek word used here, as well as the Latin translation of St. Jerome.

4. Ven. Cardinal John Henry Newman, while still a Protestant, observed this fact when he wrote: "The Church of Rome can consult expedience more freely than other bodies [i.e., Protestant churches], as trusting to her living tradition, and is sometimes thought to disregard principle and scruple [i.e., change its teachings], when she is but dispensing with forms" (*An Essay on the Development of Christian Doctrine* 5:3:5).

5. For a list of the relevant Bible passages that demonstrate this, see my book *Where Is That in the Bible?* (Huntington, Ind.: Our Sunday Visitor Publishing, 2001), 47-57.

6. Cf. CCC 249-256.

7. The Greek noun form for tradition, *paradosis*, is used here. This is the same word used by Christ in Matthew 15:1-9, where he condemns erroneous, bad traditions of men that "nullify the word of God." Later in this book we will discuss the distinction between the bad traditions Christ condemned and the holy Traditions, which are from God, as well as those traditions of men that are good and helpful and not contrary to God's commandments.

8. We must be clear that while the Church's "small-t" traditions (customs and disciplines) are in themselves not doctrinal (i.e., not part of divine revelation), they have a doctrinal dimension in that they reflect or express certain doctrinal truths. For example, the Catholic practice of blessing oneself with holy water is not doctrinal, but it very aptly expresses the doctrinal fact of baptismal regeneration.

9. The Greek compound word St. Paul used here for "inspired" was *theopneustos*, which literally means "God-breathed."

10. Some versions, such as the Revised Standard Version (RSV), omit the words "and fasting" (Greek: *kai nesteia;* Latin: *et ieiunio*) in Mark 9:29. Other major versions, such as St. Jerome's Latin Vulgate, the Douay-Rheims, and the King James Version contain the phrase "and fasting."

11. That is, a Church council or a Church Father, usually a bishop or an early pope.

12. That is, protected by God from formally teaching error. For an in-depth biblical and historical explanation of this key Catholic Tradition, see my book *Pope Fiction: Answers to 30 Myths and Misconceptions About the Papacy*, Basilica Press, 1999.

13. Our Sunday Visitor Publishing, 2001.

14. Cf. Matthew 16:18. For many more Scripture passages on this subject, see my book *Where Is That in the Bible?*

15. That is, to allege that their doctrines were present in the apostolic age.

16. Cf. Matthew 16:18.
17. Cf. John 21:17.
18. That is, "cathedras."
19. Cf. 2 Timothy 4:21.
20. Cf. Philippians 4:3.
21. Cf. Romans 1:8.
22. Referring to the sacrament of confession.
23. Cf. Matthew 16:18.
24. That is, the Diocese of Rome.
25. "His name" here refers to Kepha (cf. John 1:40-42; Matthew 16:18) or "rock," which was translated into Greek as *Petros* and into English as Peter.
26. That is, written by Pope Leo the Great, cited above.
27. Known as the "quartodeciman controversy."
28. This episode is recounted in some detail for us by Eusebius of Caesarea in his *Ecclesiastical History* 5:23:1—24:11.
29. That is, the notorious heretic.
30. Dionysius is here addressing himself to Pope Soter, bishop of Rome at that time.
31. From what we can gather from Eusebius's *Ecclesiastical History*, which speaks about Caius at some length, it appears he was either a Roman priest or a learned lay apologist.
32. That is, "Rock" (Aramaic: *Kepha*); cf. John 1:40-42; Matthew 16:18; 1 Corinthians 15:5.
33. Cf. Matthew 16:18-19.
34. That is, the bishop of Hieropolis, Egypt, circa A.D. 120.
35. A.D. 150.
36. A.D. 190.
37. Cf. 2 Peter 3:15-17.
38. Referring here to the canon of the Old Testament, on which there was some dispute, even among eminent Catholic theologians, such as Athanasius, Jerome, and others, as to the extent of the canon and whether the Deuterocanonical books (see following footnote) should be admitted.

39. That is, the seven books of the Old Testament (Sirach, Tobit, Wisdom, Baruch, Judith, and 1 and 2 Maccabees, as well as sections of Esther and Daniel) that are commonly known as the "Deuterocanonical" books.

40. Sadly, in spite of his erudition and brilliance, Tertullian lapsed into the Montanist heresy toward the end of his life and died estranged from the Church in schism.

41. For the biblical passages in question, see my book *Where Is That in the Bible?*

42. Cf. Isaiah 9:6; Matthew 1:23; Luke 1:32, 35, 43; 2:11; Galatians 4:4.

43. Cf. Epistle 9, to Anysius, bishop of Thessalonica.

44. Cf. John 1:14.

45. Ibid.

46. The Latin word *cultus* (meaning "a reverent or respectful attention to") does not have any of the negative, pejorative connotations that the English word "cult" does in modern usage. And Dr. Kelly is here using the term "cult of martyrs" (Latin: *cultus martyrorum*) in the classical sense, meaning the movement among Christians to venerate these heroes. Don't let the very different and pejorative sense of the modern term "cult" throw you off here.

47. J.N.D. Kelley, *Early Christian Doctrines* (New York: Harper Collins, 1978), 409.

48. For an expanded discussion of the biblical evidence for purgatory, see my book *Where Is That in the Bible?*

49. Cf. Pope Pius XII's encyclical *Mystici Corporis Christi*.

50. By "sacrifices" Tertullian refers here to the *sacrifice of the Mass*, offered for the repose of the souls of deceased Christians.

51. Cf. Job 1:5.

52. That is, the mercy of prayers on their behalf.

53. That is, the Eucharistic sacrifice.

54. Cf. *Didache* 9:5.

55. Cf. Matthew 28:19.

56. Cf. 2 Kings 5:14.

57. Cf. Mark 10:38.

58. Cf. Romans 6:3; Colossians 2:12-13.

59. See also Tertullian, *On Baptism*, 7:1, 12:1; St. Cyril of Jerusalem, *Catechetical Lectures* 19.

60. For a fuller discussion of the biblical foundations for this doctrine and some fifty others that are often disputed by Protestants and other non-Catholics, see my book *Where Is That in the Bible?* (Huntington, Ind.: Our Sunday Visitor Publishing, 2001).

61. Which is a direct parallel to the Lord's bestowal on Simon Peter (first) and all the apostles of the power and authority to "bind and loose" on earth and in heaven.

62. That is, Sunday.

63. This is one of the classic passages that demonstrate the validity and importance of Christian Tradition.

64. Cf. Matthew 5:23-24.

65. Cf. Malachi 1:11, 14.

66. Note that several verses earlier, in John 6:11, we read how Christ fed the masses with a miraculous multiplication of bread at the time of Passover. The Last Supper, where the Lord instituted and delivered to his Church the gift of the Eucharist, which he foretold here in John 6, took place on the feast of Passover. We're told in John 6 that after having given thanks (Greek: *eucharistásas,* from the root form *eucharisteo*, and from which we derive the English word "Eucharist"), Christ performed the miracle that fed thousands with only a few small loaves of bread and a few fish. The next day, after miraculously giving the people physical bread to feed them temporarily, he then taught them at length about the "bread from heaven" that would feed them for eternity (cf. John 6:34-35).

67. The term "transubstantiation" — as a precise way of describing the fact that, at the moment of Consecration, the substance of the elements of bread and wine ceased to exist and were entirely replaced with the reality (i.e., substance) of the Body and Blood, soul and divinity of Christ — was adopted in 1079 by theologian Hildebert of Tours and rapidly caught on among other

theologians. In that same year, during the reign of Pope Gregory VII, deacon Berengarious of Tours, who publicly denied Transubstantiation and had been promoting that error, took an oath affirming his belief in the orthodox definition of Transubstantiation. In 1215 the Fourth Lateran Council adopted "transubstantiation" as the definitive term used to express this Tradition. This usage was followed in 1274 by the Council of Lyons, and in 1545 by the Council of Trent. These formal definitions of the nature of the Eucharist and the Real Presence entailed that the term "transubstantiation" itself became part of the living Tradition of the Church. This does not in any way mean or imply that the doctrine of Transubstantiation was "invented" in the eleventh century. Rather, just as the technical theological term "Trinity" (Greek: *triados*, Latin: *trinitas*) was not developed by Catholic theologians until nearly the second century, the new term the Church eventually settled on was simply a better way to express the truth that had always been taught since the time of Christ and the Apostles.

68. Cf. Matthew 26:26.

69. I use the word "icon" here in a more general sense to denote sacred images, as opposed to the more technical and precise meaning of images painted on boards.

70. The Christian catacombs in Rome, for example, abound with thousands of still extant examples of these simple early Christian icons, typically carved into pieces of marble or stone and affixed to the walls and sarcophagi in the subterranean catacomb galleries. These icons, dating from the second century, are still visible today to anyone who tours the catacombs.

71. The Council of Elvira (circa A.D. 305-309) was a regional synod attended by about twenty bishops at a site near the modern-day city of Granada. A canon from this council forbade the use of lifelike painted images in churches, and this is often misinterpreted by opponents of the holy icons as a "proof" of ancient Christian opposition to icons themselves. But this is a mis-

reading of the council's intent. The synod Fathers appeared to have enacted this measure as a provisional pastoral measure to avoid the problem of local pagans mocking sacred things and to help curb any latent tendencies among Christians toward any misuse of sacred images that could drift toward idolatry. Russian Orthodox art historian N. Pokrovsky observed, "The apologists [of the early second century] say nothing about a Christian opposition in principle against images, but only testify that images were very few in number in their times. And this is true. [For] if Christians had not favored sacred representations, we would not have monuments of Christian art from the first centuries found in exactly those places where Christians met [e.g., the catacombs in Rome]. At the same time, the enormous diffusion of images in the course of the following centuries would be incomprehensible and inexplicable if they had not existed before" (Leonid Ouspensky, *Theology of the Icon* [Crestwood, N.Y.: St. Vladimir's Seminary Press, 1978], 44-45).

72. One can reasonably assume that there were many thousands more of these early Christian icons that were destroyed or lost through natural decay over the last nineteen centuries.

73. At the conclusion of preaching his sermon praising the heroic virtue of the martyr St. Barlaam.

74. Leonid Ouspensky, *Theology of the Icon* (Crestwood, N.Y.: St. Vladimir's Seminary Press, 1978), 41.

75. Dramatic evidence showing the universal practice of venerating the saints and martyrs in early Christian art is seen in the decorations and architecture of many still-extant ancient Catholic basilicas and churches; cf. Yoram Tsafrir, ed., *Ancient Churches Revealed* (Jerusalem: Israel Exploration Society, 1993).

76. Henri Daniel-Rops, *The Church of Apostles and Martyrs* (London: J. M. Dent & Sons, Ltd., 1960), 401.

77. Herbert Thurston, in his article on "Relics," *The Catholic Encyclopedia* (New York: Robert Appleton Co., 1911), vol. 12.

78. St. Cyril refers here to the miraculous episode in 2 Kings 13 in which the bones of the Prophet Elisha raised to life the corpse of a man who was about to be buried and which merely touched the bones of Elisha.

79. Augustine pleaded with Petilianus: "[M]ay God separate you from the party of Donatus [i.e., the Donatist heresy], and call you back again into the Catholic Church, whence you were torn by them while you were still a catechumen" (*Response to the Letters of Petilianus, the Donatist* 2:105, circa A.D. 398).

80. Ibid., 2:38, 90–91.

81. Both in the general meaning of "orthodox," as well as its specific meaning of a particular, visible Church.

82. Cf. 1 John 3:10.

83. Cf. James 3:8.

84. Cf. 1 Peter 5:8.

85. That is, turning away from the Tradition of the "fathers" of the Church; the Apostles and their disciples, indeed all those bishops who handed on the Tradition of the Apostles, which Eutyches had abandoned through heresy.

86. Cf. p. 161.

87. Cf. Matthew 27:45–47; Mark 15:34.

88. Cf. Acts 3:1.

89. This section on novenas is adapted from a longer article I wrote in the December, 1989, issue of the *Catholic Answers* apologetics newsletter.

90. "The word for Christmas in late Old English is *Cristes Maesse*, the Mass of Christ, first found in 1038, and *Cristes-messe*, in 1131. In Dutch it is *Kerst-misse*, in Latin *Dies Natalis*, whence comes the French *Noël*, and Italian *Il natale*; in German *Weihnachtsfest*, from the preceding sacred vigil" (*The Catholic Encyclopedia* [New York, Robert Appleton Co., 1908], vol. 3, p. 724.

91. Cf. *Homilies on Leviticus* 8.

92. As quoted in the *Catholic Encyclopedia*, vol. 3, p. 725.

93. Catholic writer T. Slater explains how the names

of the days of the week developed: "Sunday (Day of the Sun), as the name of the first day of the week, is derived from Egyptian astrology. The seven planets, known to us as Saturn, Jupiter, Mars, the Sun, Venus, Mercury, and the Moon, each had an hour of the day assigned to them, and the planet which was regent during the first hour of any day of the week gave its name to that day. During the first and second century the week of seven days was introduced into Rome from Egypt, and the Roman names of the planets were given to each successive day. The Teutonic nations seem to have adopted the week as a division of time from the Romans, but they changed the Roman names into those of corresponding Teutonic deities. Hence the *dies Solis* [Latin: 'day of the Sun'] became Sunday (German: *Sonntag*). Sunday was the first day of the week according to the Jewish method of reckoning, but for Christians it began to take the place of the Jewish Sabbath in Apostolic times as the day set apart for the public and solemn worship of God" (*The Catholic Encyclopedia* [New York: Robert Appleton Co., 1912], vol. 14, p. 335).

94. Also known as "The Lord's Teaching Through the Twelve Apostles to the Nations."

95. For a popular, concise explanation of the relationship between the Eucharistic Liturgy and the Book of Revelation, see Scott Hahn, *The Lamb's Supper* (New York: Doubleday, 1999).

96. Cf. CCC 2064-2068.

97. Keep in mind that both the issue of circumcision and keeping the Lord's Day holy are *direct commands from God*. Catholics should be aware that sometimes Seventh-Day Adventists will attempt to defend their error by saying that the Ten Commandments are somehow more inviolable than the commandment from God to Abraham regarding circumcision. But that is an invalid argument. Both commandments came directly from God, both were recorded in Scripture, and the command to perform circumcision was given, chronologically, well before the Ten Commandments were given.

98. The English phrase "to the close of the age" is more accurately rendered "until the consummation of the ages" or "until the end of the world" (cf. St. Jerome's Latin translation [*usque ad consummationem saeculi*] of the Greek phrase *heos tes sunteleias tou aionos*).

99. *The Catholic Encyclopedia* (New York: Robert Appleton Co., 1908), vol. 8, pp. 785-786.

100. Pronounced *DID-ah-kay*.

101. In patristic writings, the word "apology" means the exact opposite of our modern-day usage of that word. These days, an "apology" is an expression of remorse or regret, an effort to exculpate oneself for having done something wrong. This is not how the word was used in the early Church. The classical meaning of an apology is a *defense*. It connotes a robust effort to vindicate one's position, not to repent of it.

102. Cf. Exodus 22:18.

103. "Ever since St. Augustine, the Ten Commandments have occupied a predominant place in the catechesis of baptismal candidates and the faithful. In the fifteenth century, the custom arose of expressing the commandments of the Decalogue in rhymed formulae, easy to memorize and in positive form. They are still in use today. The catechisms of the Church have often expounded Christian morality by following the order of the Ten Commandments" (CCC 2065).

104. John H. Stapleton, *The Catholic Encyclopedia* (New York: Robert Appleton Co., 1908), vol. 4, pp. 153-154.

ABOUT THE AUTHOR

Patrick Madrid is the publisher of the award-winning *Envoy* magazine, a leading journal of Catholic apologetics and evangelization — www.envoymagazine. com.

He is a best-selling author whose books include the *Surprised by Truth* series, *Pope Fiction*, *Where Is That in the Bible?*, and *Search and Rescue: How to Bring Your Family and Friends Into — or Back Into — the Catholic Church.* He is a contributor to the forthcoming Ignatius Press *Encyclopedia of Catholic Apologetics.*

Patrick is also the host of two EWTN television series: "Pope Fiction" and "The Truth About Scripture and Tradition." He has conducted hundreds of apologetics and evangelization conferences in English and Spanish across the U.S., as well as throughout Europe, Asia, and in Latin America. He is a veteran of numerous formal public debates with Protestant ministers, Mormon leaders, and other non-Catholic spokesmen.

He and his wife Nancy have been blessed with eleven children.

For information about Patrick's popular apologetics seminars and speaking schedule, please visit www.surprisedbytruth.com. You can contact him at: P.O. Box 640, Granville, OH 43023. Fax: 740-928-5975. E-mail: patrick@surprisedbytruth.com.

Our Sunday Visitor. . .
Your Source for Discovering
the Riches of the Catholic Faith

Our Sunday Visitor has an extensive line of materials for young children, teens, and adults. Our books, Bibles, booklets, CD-ROMs, audios, and videos are available in bookstores worldwide.

To receive a FREE full-line catalog or for more information, call **Our Sunday Visitor** at **1-800-348-2440**. Or write, **Our Sunday Visitor** / 200 Noll Plaza / Huntington, IN 46750.

- -

Please send me: ___A catalog

Please send me materials on:

___Apologetics and catechetics   ___Reference works

___Prayer books   ___Heritage and the saints

___The family   ___The parish

Name_____

Address_____Apt._____

City_____State_____Zip_____

Telephone (   ) _____

                                                 A23BBABP

- -

Please send a friend: ___A catalog

Please send a friend materials on:

___Apologetics and catechetics   ___Reference works

___Prayer books   ___Heritage and the saints

___The family   ___The parish

Name_____

Address_____Apt._____

City_____State_____Zip_____

Telephone (   ) _____

                                                 A23BBABP

- -

Our Sunday Visitor
200 Noll Plaza
Huntington, IN 46750
Toll free: 1-800-348-2440
E-mail: osvbooks@osv.com
Website: www.osv.com